MEDITATIONS ON LONELINESS

The Worst Kind of Pain

by

Paul Thomas Sharp

ISBN-10: 1-4810-2122-2
ISBN-13: 978-1-48-102122-7

PART ONE:
A THEOLOGY OF LONELINESS

PART TWO:
SKETCHES OF LONELINESS

ACKNOWLEDGEMENTS

I would like to express my thanks to those who inspired this work and those who assisted in its production. Foremost among these is Shea Ashworth. Following the death of her dear husband and servant of Christ, Dick Ashworth in August 2005, Shea was gracious enough to receive my phone calls regarding her well-being. It was on one of those occasions that she uttered the words that form the subtitle of this book—"*loneliness is the worst kind of pain.*" Shea, your words went straight to my heart and grabbed my attention with all ten fingers and forced me to ask a question of God's Word that I had not asked up until that time. You and Dick let me into your private times so easily and graciously during the last several months and I thank you for that. But your giving has continued and the transparent statement you made, without, I suppose, expecting any response, has resulted in this. Whether it helps or only muddies the waters even more, only time and God will determine. I do know for sure that the search has not lessened loneliness in my vocabulary nor made it the most important thing to understand and deal with. Instead, your statement has made me examine God by the pain of your experience to see if He is Who I believed Him to be from His word. I am sure that He is the Father of mercies and the God of all comfort (2 Cor. 1:3, 4).

A second person also prodded me in this direction at the same time as Shea. I will omit the name for privacy reasons but this person spoke to me over the phone with brokenness about the loneliness felt by those who have gone through divorce. To you, my friend, and to all those like you, I offer this attempt to answer your frustrations and emptiness. I don't expect my words to fill the void. I do expect God to honor His promises and character to not forsake anyone who seeks Him, who waits on Him, who shares all life's vicissitudes with Him (Psalm 9:9, 10; 22:23, 24; 27:14; 31:24).

May the readers, O God, who venture upon You find that as painful as our loneliness may be, it is not as painful as it could be if You did not oversee it, restrain it, enter into it and sanctify it, even including it in Your original design for Your creation. It is my prayer that something said in this work, either by me or by others I quote, may be a bit of light in the darkness, a fragrant incense in the staleness of a locked room, and a stimulating thought to the numbed mind.

It is to God's great honor that He uses us in any way to make Himself known to others. And so I ask all who read and profit by this effort to return thanks to where thanks are due (Rom. 11:33–36).

Paul Thomas Sharp
August 20, 2007

INTRODUCTION

I asked my eye doctor one day about Macular Degeneration, since my grandfather had suffered with it the last years of his life. Calmly he began to discus the degenerative disease and gave me some things to help delay it. But quite naturally he told me about his own dad's experience with MD, sliding into a disclosure of a side effect I hadn't heard of, loneliness. For although the eyesight degenerates to nearly nothing the appearance of the eyes looks normal. So when his dad went out in public, say to a funeral visitation or a sporting event, people he had known for a long time would see him looking at them, and when they would wave or nod, he made no return, since he couldn't see them. But they mistook it for a cold shoulder, a snub and soon his dad had fewer friends calling. Gradually he wanted to go out less often, since he couldn't see and often stumbled and fell over obstacles, and the serious side of isolation, with its loss of self-worth and despair, set in.

Everywhere I go I meet lonely people, and the causes seem to be more numerous as time goes on. So it seems. The songs and literature of loneliness go back as far as any record of human experience does, and it doesn't seem that the future holds any certain cure for it either, if the present is any judge. But in the following pages I attempt to face it head on and understand why we are lonely, what, if anything, can be done to assist us in our lonely times, and lastly to stimulate you to think about these things so that you may add to what I have learned.

Your discoveries plus mine will keep us from being orphans. We will have each other, and I think we will find an adoptive Father who will fill the void like no one else can.

3

PRELUDE

Feel deeply this pain, then, my soul
since it is both unavoidable and desirable
unavoidable in that no one has found
by God's design
a permanent cure or defense
to overcome it
desirable in that it is loneliness
alone,
which can lead to pure joy at the endless fellowship
and communion yet to come
So feel this pain, my soul
as deeply as it may pierce
at very worst, my joy shall be the greater
since I have been the sadder
I will be surprised by joy
at very best, the pain can propel me forward
to the meeting time
a profitable friend is he who rouses me from my delusions and
sobers me from my drunkenness
"here is no place to stay," he says
"you have no lasting fullness here."

PART ONE:
A THEOLOGY OF LONELINESS

CHAPTER 1

LONELY BY DESIGN

Then the Lord God took the man and put him in the garden of Eden to tend and keep it. And the Lord God commanded the man, saying, "Of every tree of the garden you may freely eat; but of the tree of the knowledge of good and evil you shall not eat, for in the day that you eat of it you shall surely die." And the Lord God said, "It is not good that man should be alone; I will make him a helper comparable to him." Out of the ground the Lord God formed every beast of the field and every bird of the air, and brought them to Adam to see what he would call them. And whatever Adam called each living creature, that was its name. So Adam gave names to all cattle, to the birds of the air, and to every beast of the field. But for Adam there was not found a helper comparable to him. And the Lord God caused a deep sleep to fall on Adam, and he slept; and He took one of his ribs, and closed up the flesh in its place. Then the rib which the Lord God had taken from man He made into a woman, and He brought her to the man. And Adam said: "This is now bone of my bones, and flesh of my flesh; she shall be called woman, because she was taken out of Man." Therefore a man shall leave his father and mother and be joined to his wife, and they shall become one flesh. And they were both naked, the man and his wife, and were not ashamed.

—Genesis 2:15–25

When God created, He did so with purpose and skill. He was under no limitations other than what His divine wisdom and holiness dictated to be the best way to accomplish His ultimate purpose: displaying His glorious perfections to creatures that were suited to understand and love Him for His perfections. We have a record of His self-assessment of the work at the time of creation. After the creation of light, on day one, "God saw the light, that it was good." (1:4) At the end of each of days 3–6 we are told that He had the same assessment of His unfolding creation (1:10, 12, 18, 21, 25). His final evaluation, found in 1:31 was that "God saw everything that He had made, and, behold, it was very good."

A more particular account of this creation is given to us in Genesis 2. The human male, Adam, was made first (2:7) and put in a position of oversight and responsibility for the garden of Eden (2:8, 15). In 2:18 God spoke about Adam, not to Adam, when He asserted that, "*It is not good that man should be alone.*" Compare God's previous assessment of creation and His assessment of Adam's solitary estate. It seems to me that "*good* " and "*not good*" in these passages looks not at moral good and evil but refers to appropriateness or suitableness to God's ultimate purpose. In other words, each of the statements affirming the goodness of the day's work are looking at the suitableness of what had been done, in view of what it was meant to do or be in the overall picture God was painting. Thus, light was good because it brought life giving warmth and illumination necessary for the rest of God's creatures. Each of the things or beings God created fit into the whole scheme of what He was ultimately doing (see Rom. 8:28f). Everything except man! In the eyes of the only One who mattered, Adam was not in a good or suitable state, since he was alone and lonely.

Why, then, did God, in His wisdom, create what He knew to be inadequate or unsuitable from the outset? And after announcing His assessment of Adam's solitude (2:18) why did God set him about the task of naming the animals? (2:18, 19) Was He hoping that maybe the other creatures would fill the emptiness Adam felt? Did He think that the animals could fulfill Adam and achieve the "good" label the rest of creation had in His eyes? Was God experimenting?

7

The animals did not remove Adam's loneliness. They did not fill the void he had or provide the companion he needed to fulfill the role God had created him to occupy as steward of God's creation. He had no partner to continue the species; no fellow of his stature to converse with; no one to watch over and be watched over by; no other being of spirit and flesh to be amphibious with him in a world populated by animals and plants and overshadowed by angels of pure spirit (2:20).

Was God experimenting? Does He experiment? If He did or does, what does that say about Him? What did all of this animal-naming business accomplish? (People still try to replace human companionship with animal or plant substitutes, don't they?) Did God really think that Adam's need could be met in this way? Couldn't He have made Adam complete from the first? Was He who made the countless hosts of angels in one creative act not powerful or wise enough to create a being that was self-contained and self-sufficient from the start?

The next step God took to address Adam's loneliness was to create the female, Eve (2:21). But she came at a price! Adam underwent divine surgery and lost a rib from which God fabricated another human being. Unlike the creation of Adam, Eve was made from living tissue and although she was like Adam, she was also different enough to provide the two things he needed—understanding and distinction. She was not a clone or a mirror image of himself, else he would just be talking to himself in the mirror all the time. But she was human, and could contemplate and reason and fellowship with him in every way like no other being.

Adam's response to the animals God had brought to him was to name them (2:20). Naming things is an act of describing the traits of the object and of asserting the right of authority over the object. Naming the animals was the act of a master, an official. But when Eve is presented to this solitary gardener he not only names her but embraces her as his own flesh and bone (2:23; 3:20), predicting that his posterity will perpetuate his example by men leaving their families and embracing their wives, achieving wholeness or perfect union thereby. I guess we could say that God's solution to Adam's problem was well received!

His name for her identifies her as coming from him, a fact clearly visible in the Hebrew original. But when he named her Adam did not identify her by her appearance or some other trait, nor did he name her in lordship over her, although he was her head (1Cor. 11:2–16; 1Tim. 2:8–15). Rather, he seems to find the fact that she was once part of him, was removed from him, and then returned to him as the most significant fact about her. Her name, *"woman"*, is like saying "Welcome back," and "My, how different and better you are than when you were just my rib."

Let's summarize what we have seen.

Everything Was Good...Almost

Before sin came into the world (Gen. 3) God's creation was good (fitting or suitable for what He made it for). This included the vast diversity of creation (plants, animals, non-living matter, heavenly objects) and a vast number of beings, in different genders, that were to reproduce after their kind, for the ongoing support of life on earth (1:11,12, 20–25). All living things, except Adam, had a suitable opposite to partner with and fill the earth, as God had commanded. Only Adam was created alone, and his aloneness was not good, in God's estimation. We may guess that Adam agreed with that verdict. He felt alone, with none of his kind anywhere in existence! **He was lonely by design.**

The Only Lonely One

The obvious differences between himself and all other life forms were made plain to Adam by his task of naming the beings with whom he shared the planet. God made him feel his absolute uniqueness so as to bring him to the same conclusion He had about Adam's condition. It was not due to an oversight on God's part or a deficiency in His power that Adam was not *"good"* in his solitude. It was an intentional part of God's wise and holy design, because Adam was not like anything else in all of creation, even the angels. Even they had companions—fellow angels—to assist them in God's designed purpose for them. But Adam, of all creation, was alone out of respect to his nature, purpose and in order to best glorify God in the manner of His provision for that loneliness. In no other way could God receive the esteem He deserved than by making Adam solitary, convincing him of his need, and then providing his need by taking his own tissue and producing a perfect but different likeness of himself to complete his lack.

Wooed to Want

God's method of bringing Adam to the realization of his solitude is highly illuminating about God's methods of dealing with mankind as a whole, versus all other creatures. Mankind is brought to want what God wants. He is persuaded by experience and reason to desire what God wants to give him. By means of naming the animals and discovering that he was alone, Adam agreed with God's assessment of his condition and became a willing contributor to the solution, instead of a mindless or rebellious captive that must be knocked down and forcefully made to give up a rib, for his own good. After all, had God exhausted His ability to create other humans like Adam? Could He not have made another one, a female, by the same method as He had made Adam? His methods reveal that Adam and all mankind occupy a unique place in God's program, a place that dictates that He treat them in accordance with their nature as rational and willful beings. When Adam was brought to agreement with God's opinion he wanted what God had designed to meet his need and he submitted to that remedy. As a result, Adam was fulfilled, Eve gets life, mankind had a future and God is praised more than if He had done otherwise or by other means (Philippians 1:3–6; 2:12–13).

There is abundant food for thought here regarding God's other dealings with mankind, especially His method of saving people from sin's devastating rule. The process of conviction, repentance and conversion leading to salvation follows the same pattern as Adam's finding fulfillment in Eve. And all along, it is God at work. But He brings us to want what we need, which He has provided for, in His wisdom, power and goodness by a road that reflects our design, as image bearers of God. His ways with us in our salvation are through the power of the gospel to reason with us, to reveal to us what our consciences and experiences affirm is true. The gracious Spirit patiently woos and follows us down every alley we try, reminding us of our emptiness, until we have a desire to submit to His provision—a God-made completion to our void.

A Legacy of Loneliness

Adam's prophecy of mankind's perpetual "leaving" and "cleaving" points out the fact that loneliness was to be an ongoing part of the human experience, irregardless of sin, and family was going to be both the source of companionship for young humans and the springboard from which lonely people would launch out to find their own completeness in someone who is like them but is also different. By God's design, Adam's experience of loneliness has been repeated countless times, by all of his progeny.

Born into a family where they would be cherished and cared for, they would inevitably become lonely for something their family could not provide. This sense of incompleteness and need would be the necessary preparative for God's provision of a suitable partner. The loneliness would be the hunger, the thirst, and the pain that would drive them to want what He wanted for them. And when they found that provision and began their own family, the cycle would continue with their children! The parents of the cherished children would be left behind, lonely. Many would leave the family but never find a suitable helper, aggravating their loneliness even more. Many would leave those that they had come to cleave to and go wandering in search of another companion to fill the loneliness. Many would have to part, suddenly or slowly, from their partner at death, and find themselves naming animals and growing plants, alone. Once again, in view of these facts, we are forced to inquire into God's wisdom, goodness, and power. As we do so let me make one more observation.

Only a Partial Remedy

Eve did not remove all of Adam's loneliness (Ecclesiastes 3:1–13; 7:13,14). Adam was created to need God. All of the other needs Adam had were supplied by God, in His goodness, wisdom and power. God did not intend Eve to be the ultimate remedy for Adam's loneliness and, indeed, it was impossible that she could have been. Mankind was made to need God. None of His created provisions could supplant Him as the only truly fulfilling object in Adam's life. Even before the fall occurred, with its alienation and cosmic disturbance, mankind was in a state of incompleteness and want that only God could fill. Whether it was food, environment or physical companionship, God alone could be God to His creation.

Conclusions on Loneliness

So there are two general reasons for the perpetual loneliness we experience.

Reason #1: Loneliness Is a Healthy Longing for God

God created man lonely, by design, to bring him to want Himself, to love Him, to glorify Him for His glorious virtues (power, wisdom, goodness, etc.). This is a reflection of God's greatness and mankind's unique place in creation, for he alone was designed to be reasoned with, to be persuaded to come willingly to want what God wants for him and to submit to God's authority and all-sufficiency. Even in company with his perfect human equivalent, Adam still needed God. In fact, Eve made Adam more dependent and needy than if he had no wife! Now he had an individual to protect and factor into his plans. He must learn how to share, negotiate, be selfless, and raise children together with another autonomous being. While Eve was a welcome supply for some of his needs she could never displace Adam's innate need and dependence on God. Whenever he had a need, that need was a summons to find his sufficiency in God, the all-sufficient One. God alone knows no loneliness.

Reason #2: Loneliness Is an Indication of Our Separation from God

Mankind's sin has magnified and aggravated the original, designed loneliness by alienating us from God, darkening our understanding, perverting our emotions and exposing us to being pillaged by the world, the flesh and the devil (Ephesians 4:17–20). When Adam chose to reject God's law he rejected God as his overlord, breaking the designed loneliness-supply formula God had created. In other words, what Adam did in taking from the tree that God had prohibited is the same as if he had rejected God's assessment of his loneliness and refused to submit to having his rib removed to make Eve. If he had rejected the conclusion that he was lonely and that no animal or plant could suffice, and then had chosen to remain alone or to attempt to make one of the other creatures his companion, that rebellion would have been an act of treason and an insult to the wisdom, goodness and power of God, just as the incident at the tree of the knowledge of good and evil was. But in rebelling against God at the tree, Adam was doubly guilty, since God's original goodness and kindness to him in creating him and placing him as head of the earthly order, with all of his needs provided, had been augmented by the provision of a perfect companion to fill his loneliness and enable him to carry out God's purposes for his life. His refusal to submit to God, after all of God's lavish goodness, was the height of insolence and disrespect.

Whereas Adam had predicted that his offspring would follow his experience of:

- Starting life secure in a family unit and in fellowship with God
- Becoming lonely for companionship, but still in fellowship with God

- Being fulfilled by human companionship and the fellowship of God

because of his sin, his offspring would follow his fallen experience of . . .

- Starting life alienated from God and part of an alienated human family.
- Becoming lonely for companionship while alienated from God
- Possibly fulfilled by human companionship but still alienated from God

Whereas Eve was the complement to a need Adam had, as designed by God, she was not all that Adam needed. Creation cannot survive without the Creator. He cannot be substituted for or replaced. If He is alienated, that lack has no adequate replacement. All of the supplemental things He has made to meet our needs will fail to meet the need we have for Him. It is like putting articles of value into a bag with no bottom. They inevitably fall through and shatter on the hard, cold ground.

What we have now, since Genesis 3 is double loneliness: *designed loneliness*, which was meant to find fulfillment in God's provision of companionship; and *fallen loneliness*, which has destroyed the foundation of all created fulfillment by alienating God from all friendly and loving fellowship with us. In other words, think of Adam, created alone and knowing it, feeling keenly his isolation in every direction he looks in the creation over which he rules. Then think of him with no Creator to put him to sleep and make someone to fulfill his lonely life. Do you see his double isolation? He is not only without someone like him, to supplement his emptiness, he is without a Creator to take his plight to heart and provide for his needs. His whole world is a constant, silent scream, "You have no one, no One!"

"Now this fair tree, of which he was forbidden to eat, taught him the same lesson; that his happiness lay not in enjoyment of the creatures, for there was a lacking even in paradise: so that the

forbidden tree was, in effect, the hand of the creatures, pointing many away from themselves to God for happiness. It was a sign of emptiness hung before the door of creation, with the inscription, 'This is not your rest.'" [1]

Reflections

1. Can one be lonely in a crowd? Explain your answer.

2. Can one be lonely while enjoying good health, a great marriage and a wonderful home life? Explain your answer.

3. What other words do you associate with the word "lonely"?

4. Understanding that God built loneliness into mankind's nature has the following affects upon me.

---

[1] Thomas Boston, *Human Nature in its Fourfold State*, (Bungay: C. Brightly and Co., 1807), pp. 15–16.

5. The worst part of feeling lonely is . . .

6. If I have heard you correctly…

>   …*then I should not aim at eradicating loneliness in this lifetime. Instead, I should strive to realize a balance between contentment and discontentment (Philippians 4:10–13; 1 Timothy 6:6–19).*

>   …*then a sense of loneliness or dislocation is divinely designed to bring one to greater satisfaction and worship of Him who gives the hunger and the supply.*

>   …*then I should see these truths elsewhere in the scriptures. I have found the following supporting scriptures:*

>   …*then (write down other conclusions you have made):*

Previews

1. Am I to conclude that every person has to have a human companion, a mate, in order to be fulfilled?

2. Does the alienation from God brought into the world by Adam's sin and multiplied by all of the sins of mankind (including my own) mean that God is completely absent from His creation?

3. Did Adam's sin surprise God? Is human history, including my own, something He did not reckon on? Is He in the position of reacting to what happens or is what happens part of His design?

INTERLUDE

A LETTER TO MISS D——

John Newton

There is hardly any thing in which the Lord permits me to meet with more disappointment, than in the advantage I am ready to promise myself from creature-converse. When I expect to meet any of my Christian friends, my thoughts usually travel much faster than my body: I anticipate the hour of meeting, and my imagination is warmed with expectation of what I shall say, and what I shall hear; and sometimes I have had seasons for which I ought to be more thankful than I am. It is pleasant indeed when the Lord favours us with a happy hour, and is pleased to cause our hearts to burn within us while we are speaking of his goodness.

But often it is far otherwise with me. I carry with me a dissipation of spirit, and find that I can neither impart nor receive. Something from within or from without crosses my schemes, and when I retire I seem to have gained nothing but a fresh conviction, that we can neither help nor be helped, unless the Lord himself is pleased to help us. With his presence in our hearts, we might be comfortable and happy if shut up in one of the cells of Newgate: without it, the most select company, the most desirable opportunities', prove but clouds without water.

I have sometimes thought of asking you, whether you find that difference between being abroad and at home that I do? But I take it for granted that you do not; your connections and intimacies are, I believe, chiefly with those who are highly favoured of the Lord, and if

18

you can break through or be upon your guard against the inconveniences which attend frequent changes and much company, you must be very happy in them.

But I believe, considering my weakness, the Lord has chosen wisely and well for me, in placing me in a state of retirement, and not putting it in my power, were it ever so much my inclination, to be often abroad. As I stir so seldom, I believe when I do it is not, upon the whole, to my disadvantage; for I meet with more or less upon which my reflections afterwards may, by his blessing, be useful to me, though at the time my visits most frequently convince me how little wisdom or skill I have in improving time and opportunities. But were I to live in London, I know not what might be the consequence. Indeed I need not puzzle myself about it, as my call does not lie there; but I pity and pray for those who do live there; and I admire such of them as, in those circumstances which appear so formidable to me, are enabled to walk simply, humbly, and closely with the Lord. They remind me of Daniel, unhurt in the midst of lions, or of the bush which Moses saw, surrounded with flames, yet not consumed, because the Lord was there. Some such I do know, and I hope you are one of the number.

This is certain, that if the light of God's countenance, and communion with him in love, afford the greatest happiness we are capable of, then whatever tends to indispose us for this pursuit, or to draw a veil between him and our souls, must be our great loss. If we walk with him, it must be in the path of duty, which lies plain before us when our eye is single, and we are waiting with attention upon his word, Spirit, and providence. Now, wherever the path of duty leads we are safe; and it often does lead and place us in such circumstances as no other consideration would make us choose. We were not designed to he mere recluses, but have all a part to act in life. Now, if I find myself in the midst of things disagreeable enough in themselves to the spiritual life; yet if, when the question occurs, What dost thou here? My heart can answer, I am here by the will of God; I believe it to be, all things considered, my duty to be here at this time, rather than elsewhere. If, I say, I am tolerably satisfied of this then I would not burden and grieve myself about what I cannot avoid or alter, but endeavor to take all such things up with cheerfulness, as a part of my daily cross; since I am called, not only to do the will of God, but to suffer it. But if I am doing my own will rather than his, then I have reason to fear, lest I should meet with either a snare or a sting at every step. May the Lord Jesus be with you! I am, John Newton.[2]

NEVER ALONE

Rich Mullins

"No man is an island, entire of itself,
every man is a piece of the continent, a part of the main."

"This phrase—both troublesome and comforting, yet beautiful for the power of its straightforward witness of truth—is attributed to John Donne. He may have been quoting someone else when he penned it and made this wording permanent, but even if he didn't get the words from someone else, the ideas are certainly implicit in Paul's letters and John's Gospel. Wherever it originated, this famous line has had an enduring impact on western civilization—our political philosophies, our theology, our arts, commerce and culture.

So what is hard to understand then is this: if we are not islands, why do we feel so alone? If we are "part of the main," why are we so often in a condition of isolation? Why is it that in spite of—or sometimes, more tragically, because of—our most gut-wrenching efforts to experience a sense of belonging and to participate in the sharing of camaraderie or friendship or love, we experience a deep, disturbing alienation? The sense of aloneness permeates our existence. Sometimes it subtly, almost imperceptibly crouches in the shadows—sometimes it dominates, ruthlessly marching like Sherman across every front of our lives.

---

[2] Letter by John Newton, Written to Miss D**** on January 10, 1775. (Available online at www.puritansermons.com/newton/Newt_m4 .htm.)

Why? Or more important (and more disturbing), why would any answer to this question give us little or no consolation? Why does "knowing why" offer so little relief? Why is it that we were created with a need for explanations that pales beside our need to belonging? Why are all the answers—so easy to get, to give, figure out or make up—so hard to give, to find, to share, so impossible to take—so necessary for a satisfying life?

I cannot answer this. What I do know is that, feel it or not—no man is an island, we are not alone. My failures, my successes, my strengths, and weaknesses reach beyond me—they affect people around me. Whether or not I feel close, my life—every life—touches other lives. We are joined together in a responsibility to make this world a good one for all of us. Each of us warms the world or chills it inasmuch as we offer or withhold respect, hospitality, encouragement, love or truth. In that sense we are all parts of each other's well-being or sickness, and we affect the climate that we all share.

But we are also alone. "Each heart knows its own bitterness, and none else can share its joy." (Proverbs 14:10) We each have some identity that is separate (and that separates us) from the community. We are individuals, unique in ourselves. We are responsible for our choices, capable of amazing creativity, loved by the God who made us, who redeemed us and wrote our names—not the names given us by others, but the names given (to) us by our Creator—on a white stone to be given on the other side (Rev. 2:17).

So let us love one another, enjoy each other's company, share in the common work, endure each other's failures. This will not cure our aloneness, so let's not ask that of each other. **Let's learn to not be afraid of a very necessary aloneness.** With others and without them we are at home. In both their company and our solitude we will meet God."[3]

---

[3] Rich Mullins, "Never Alone," *Release*, March–April 1996.

CHAPTER 2

HEADWATERS AND TAILWATERS

"We live, in fact, in a world starved for solitude, silence, and private: and therefore starved for meditation and true friendship."

—C. S. Lewis, *The Weight of Glory*

"We are born helpless. As soon as we are fully conscious we discover loneliness."

—C. S. Lewis, *Transposition and Other addresses*

One of the most significant events in human history to come to terms with for our understanding of ourselves as humans is **Creation**. In the first chapter we considered mankind as originally created by God, according to the Genesis record. As that study concluded, loneliness was originally built into God's design for mankind. It was to be the tool that would persuade Adam and all of his posterity of their need to embrace God's provision for them—human companionship—and to embrace His rightful place as the provider of that provision. In other words, man's necessity magnified God's sufficiency, and God's sufficiency provided for man's necessity: satisfying his need for companionship and his need to recognize that he had an all-sufficient God shepherding him (Psalm 23:1).

The second great event in human history, which we must always factor into any and all discussions on our condition, is the sin of Adam and Eve or the Fall, as it is commonly known. I have already mentioned this event briefly in chapter one but here we will spend some time looking at it more closely. Due to their unique placement in the headwaters of human history Adam and Eve introduced a factor into the original design of loneliness that has aggravated or inflamed it beyond its original design.

Headwaters

If you have fished much in your life the term *"headwaters"* may be a familiar one to you. When I lived in the Pacific Northwest two of my favorite streams, the Cedar and Green rivers, were used to supply the drinking water for the large population centers around Tacoma and Seattle. At a certain point in the course of each stream no trespassing was allowed, not even for such innocent activities as fishing. And everyone knew the best fishing must be there, since no one got to fish there! The reasoning behind this policy is obvious, isn't it? Only water from the headwater sections of these rivers is used to prevent human and industrial waste from contaminating the drinking water. If you take water out before the sources of contamination come in you have healthier water for people to use.

Adam and Eve were the headwaters of all humankind, according to the wisdom of God. He didn't make a bunch of people, like He did animals. He made one pair, investing their behavior under the covenant He made with them with a profound significance for all the "downriver" descendants they carried in their bodies. Both due to their physical/ genetic parentage and to their representative placement over God's earthly creation (Gen.1:26–31), their actions would either pollute or maintain the purity of their original righteousness for all of their offspring (Rom. 5:12–21; Eccl. 7:29).

In spite of God's universally good, abundant, and wise design and perfect suitableness of the creation to its purpose, they chose to join in the rebellion of the devil by violating the single prohibition God had justly put them under (Gen. 2:8–17).

23

The penalty or consequence attached to this aggravated treason was death, in all of its forms. Since God is life and sin is the very antithesis of God, choosing to sin is the choice of death in place of life. Death in all of its variations—spiritual, relational, intellectual, physical—entered the headwaters of mankind and into the domain God had set him over (Rom. 8:18–25). The full penalty was postponed by God's mercy and longsuffering, since they did not immediately experience physical death. But they did experience immediate consequences of their abandonment of God. Consider the comparison on the following page of life before the Fall and after the Fall.

As a summary of the appalling alteration in mankind caused by the fall, please see Genesis 6:1–8, with especial attention on verses 5 and 6! Originally God had pronounced His creation, especially man, as very good. But at this juncture God was *"sorry that He had made man on the earth, and He was grieved in His heart."* Humans no longer possessed the divine image. They now bore the image of fallen Adam (Gen. 5:1–3) which was a non-stop fountain of evil (6:5; 1Cor. 15:46–49).

When the Lord Jesus Christ was asked about divorce (Matt. 19:3), His initial answer provoked His hearers to a second question (Matt. 19:4–6). His first reply looked at marriage as originally designed in Genesis 2. In that case, divorce is out of the question, since God had constituted the man and woman one flesh. What creature could undo God's orders (19:7)? Their reply also comes from a book written by Moses, Deuteronomy 24:1–4: "If you are right, Jesus," they said, *"why did Moses command us to give a certificate of divorce and put her away?"* How did our Lord respond to this dilemma? He pointed out to them that Moses' command was actually a permission not a command (19:8) and then He observed that there was an original law which He had just stated and then an amendment to that law given through Moses. The amendment was needed due to the change in man from his original condition. *"Hardness of heart"* had come into the world (19:8) causing additional guidelines to be needed from God. This hardness is a kind of death, the sentence for sin

BEFORE THE FALL	AFTER THE FALL
All animals ate plants or plant products (Gen. 1:28–31).	Animal skins were provided to cover them (Gen. 3:21) and animal sacrifices were now required (4:2f).
Noah had both animals and food on the ark (Gen. 6:19–22; 7:1–4) but after the waters receded God authorized man to eat both plants and animals (9:1–7). Was it because the killing of animals was the product of sin and became God's temporary remedy for man's nakedness that Abel's offering was acceptable and Cain's was not? (Gen. 4:3–5; Heb.11:4)	
The animals seemed to be drawn to man before sin (Gen. 2:18–20).	After the flood the animals "dreaded" man (Gen. 9:1–3). This change occurred simultaneously with the animals becoming lawful food items. They became naturally wary of humans, who were now killing their former pets.
Man had communion with God in joyful submission (Gen. 2:15f).	Man hid from God and had to be summoned from his guilty hiding place to answer for his sin (Gen. 3:10).
Adam embraced his wife as a welcome companion and equal, a gift from God (Gen. 2:23f).	Adam blamed his wife and God for his sin (Gen. 3:12).
Childbearing was to be painless. (This conclusion grows out of Gen. 3:16.)	Childbearing was to be painful. (This conclusion grows out of Gen. 3:16.)
The man and woman were co-rulers of creation (Gen. 1:26–31).	The husband is given headship over the woman, which will be an object of conflict and discord (Gen. 3:16).
The ground was blessed so as to be abundantly and easily fruitful and productive (1:28f).	The ground was cursed so as to be difficult to work and less fruitful (3:17).
Eden, the garden paradise, was theirs to tend and enjoy (2:8–25).	They were expelled from Eden by force and prohibited from returning by angelic sentries (3:22f).

God had promised. It is spiritual death. (See Eph. 2:1–3; 4:17–19; Rom. 1:18–32 for other statements of this deadness.) Adam and Eve had brought into their posterity insensitivity, unresponsiveness, selfishness, malice and all the qualities that are the opposite to the likeness of God they once had.

What does all of this have to do with loneliness? Everything. As evidenced in the details of Genesis 3, that which God had designed and created for His glory and the good of creation, was altered by the rebellion of the creatures He had designed to shepherd creation. Now mankind ran from God instead of running to Him. They blamed each other rather than support each other. They soon were robed in the skins of innocent animals, provided as sacrificial victims by God, in a foreshadowing of events that would provide coverings for more than just bodily nakedness.

Tailwaters

Down river from Adam and Eve the effects are all too familiar. Loneliness has become magnified in all of mankind. Drawn from such polluted headwaters, we have added our own contamination to the stream. The original fellowship with God which Adam had in the garden, from which all of his loneliness had a solution, is absent at our birth (Ps. 51:5; 58:3; Rom. 3:9–18; 1 Cor. 15:20–22, 46–49). If we ignore this fact or underestimate its impact on the state of things, we will never resolve the dilemma we are in.

Do you remember the three questions I raised at the end of chapter 1?

1. Does every human have to have a mate to be fulfilled or overcome loneliness?
2. Is the alienation introduced by sin complete or final? Is God completely absent from His creation?
3. Did Adam's sin surprise God? Was it an unforeseen overturning of God's design?

Let's begin to answer these questions, for these are the tailwaters, the downriver results from that pivotal time in the

26

garden of Eden. As we go on in this study we will have occasion to add to our answers, but we can begin now to gain insights into them.

1. Did God intend for every human to have a human mate, that is, to get married?

We may never know what God "intended" to take place because sin's entrance and tragic rule introduced an element into the formula that altered the course of history. Just as Jesus told the Pharisees that *"hardness of heart"* was the reason for the apparent contradiction in God's laws for marriage and divorce, so we can observe two distinct lines of revelation about loneliness: the original, created design, and that which sin produced. All we can know for sure is what is true *since the Fall*. We have no way of knowing what would have happened had there been no Fall (see Eccl. 7:29).

His will or design for each member of Adam's race does not now include marriage for all, nor does marriage absolutely remove loneliness from those He does will to be married (Matt. 19:10–12; 1Cor. 7:6–40). The death of a marriage partner actually causes a kind of loneliness that would never have been known if there had not been a marriage in the first place.

That God intended mankind to be a social being—needing companionship from his fellow man—is still a valid reflection of the original design. No one can create his own life; sustain his own life; fulfill his own emotional, intellectual and physical needs; or dispose of his own remains when his life has ended. The Church, the body of believers in Christ, is so constructed that no one part can function without the others. The gifts and the aim of those gifts are to build up the rest of the body parts (1Cor. 12:4–31). If the new creation, devoid of sin, is a place of perfect companionship, and the society of believers at present is designed to find fulfillment and give fulfillment to its members, then we must conclude that it is God's intention for us to find some cure for our loneliness in our fellow man, especially our fellow believers.

The fact of our native evil, manifested in our continual rebelliousness from God's will, is the second greatest power source in the universe. Sin, both in angels and man, is exceeded in power only by God's greatness (Rom. 5:20, 21). With sin's influence in all of mankind, a devil at work to fuel our natural willfulness and a whole world subject to death and violence, God's original designs are manifestly marred, distorted and abused. Just as a fragment from a beautiful stained glass may be used by a vandal to focus the sun's rays and ignite a fire that then destroys a palace. God's original masterpiece is barely recognizable amid the ruins of the world as we know it. Now people resist God's holy attitude towards sexuality and disregard parental counsel about suitable marriage partners. We view others as beneath us if they don't appeal to our eyes or desirable if they do. We make our own rules about how we relate to our fellow man, and usually these rules are self-serving and sensual. We abuse creation and selfishly horde its treasures for our own short-term pleasures.

2. Is God absolutely alienated from creation? Is He absent from us?

If He were, then we would be absolutely alone and loneliness would be the only fitting condition for us; a just penalty applied rightly by a holy Judge to those who don't want Him in their lives on His terms.

Genesis 3:8f gives us the wonderful good news that God did not abandon mankind to his self-chosen abyss. Instead, He initiated a search and rescue mission.

First, He brought the cringing, arguing, finger-pointing couple out of the shadows and into the light, to the cleansing of confession.

Second, He judged their sin, in mercy and restraint befitting a God of exalted virtues (Gen. 3:14–24). Holiness and mercy kiss each other in God (Ps. 85:10–13). Notice especially Gen. 3:16–19, as it pertains to our subject. Eve, God's remedy for Adam's loneliness, is sentenced to a forced subordination to her husband, although she had led the way in the decision to disobey God. This reveals one of sin's menaces, ambition. Just as they were covetous to have the one thing God had restrained from them, so now she will have to deal continually with a restricted role in her relationship with Adam, in their God given role as earth's caregivers. They had rejected subordination to God, so they received subordination to each other in consequence (1 Tim. 2:8–15). Adam, too, no longer had the same relationship with the world as before his sin. Now, the earth would resist his efforts and ultimately he would return to the earth, in submission to the death he had introduced.

In all of the sentences the Judge handed down there is a frustration factor evident. That which God had intended was now altered, and loneliness and frustration became mankind's double portion: double because not only was there the designed loneliness God had built into mankind but there was now the complicating element of sin.

Third, God provided for their near and long-term needs. He made skin coverings to replace the plant aprons (3:21). He removed them from further and greater danger (3:22–24). He promised a deliverer, through <u>Eve's</u> seed (3:15). Note the omission of Adam in the prediction of the deliverer, which was accomplished in the virgin conception of Jesus by Mary.

God's absolute alienation or abandonment of mankind is the essence of hell. No one has been "*God forsaken*" yet. But that will change when death and Hades are cast into the lake of fire (Rev. 20:14, 15).

To sum up, God did not completely abandon His creation after Adam sinned. His alienation is not absolute but it is real. He is the offended, infinitely holy One, and it is His great power to restrain His wrath that appears most glorious in this post-Fall world. The subsequent history of redemption reveals His ongoing presence and activity among the broken shards of that once perfect stained glass window. He has undertaken to purify the *tailwaters* by diverting them into a *new headwater*—Christ.

3. Did Adam's sin surprise God? Was it an unforeseen overturning of God's design?

With the answers I have suggested for the first two questions, it is only logical then to ask this question. Since God's original design and plan has been altered by sin and since He has been alienated from sinful man, though not absolutely or completely, was the fall of man an unplanned overturning of God's work? In other words is it accurate to speak of the pre-Fall design as being God's ultimate design? Was Satan's revolt, resulting in one-third of the angels falling with him and warring with the unfallen angels an amazement to God? Is He in the position of trying to find a spare tire for His poor, wrecked creation? Was He caught off guard by the fall and so now finds Himself backpedaling, looking for the second best resolution, now that His first choice is out of the question?

Before I answer this line of questioning please reflect on how any answer will reflect on the character of God; on His reputation as being good, righteous, powerful, wise, sovereign and omniscient. As a tree is known by its fruit so God's actions provide evidence for Who He is.

Could He not have created in such a way that no angel revolted and became a subtle tempter? Could He not have made mankind tempter-proof? Could He not have guarded the forbidden tree better, as He did after Adam and Eve had eaten? Better yet, could He not have excluded the tree from the garden completely? Could He not have killed Adam and Eve immediately, in righteous judgment, thus removing the cancer from mankind and then starting over, with a fresh pair of parents? Did all of mankind have to spring from one man? Couldn't God have made many pairs of people, just in case something went wrong with one of them?

Our answers to these provocative questions can either be addressed from speculation or from revelation; either we use our own imagination, or that of some other creature, or we allow God to reveal the answers to us, in His own defense. If you believe God hasn't spoken or that there is no God to speak, the whole matter may be only mildly curious to you. However you, too, still have to deal with the undeniable realities of loneliness in an evil world, and you, too, must make some attempts to resolve this tension in order to survive the ordeal of your life, in the hopes of salvaging some measure of joy, purpose and hope to live by.

From the record of God's actions and words in Genesis 3 does God appear surprised? Was He at a loss as to what to do next? Doesn't His prohibition in 2:17 anticipate the possibility of Adam's sin? Isn't the intent of warnings and threats to deter wrong behavior and justify punishment when disobedience occurs? Don't they magnify the righteousness and wisdom of their giver and manifest the lawbreaker to be inexcusable? Someone may point to Gen. 3:11 as an indication that God was surprised or less than omniscient. But is it conceivable that the same Being who designed and created everything from nothing would not be able to know the whereabouts of the only people on earth, and they being His prized creations? Would such a Creator need an inquisition to find out that they had broken His law? Aren't God's questions rather a continuation of His method of dealing with mankind in accordance with their rational makeup, as seen before in the creation of the woman (2:18–22)? Wasn't He soliciting their confession of need and not the coordinates of their location?

What about His postponement of the full sentence of death on them at the time of their sin? What about His removal of them from the garden, wherein the tree of life continued to be dangerous to them, since it would perpetuate them in their sinful state permanently? What about the promise of a seed from the woman, not the man, that would conquer the serpent's seed? What about His provision of adequate coverings, at the cost of innocent, sacrificial animals? Do these look like stop gap, desperate, "duct-tape" solutions?

I recall sitting on my couch one day and reading the following words written by Jonathan Edwards. They took my breath away. See what effect they have on you as they address the question at hand. I have taken the liberty of highlighting Edwards' repeated use of comparative or superlative adjectives to keep this truth before your eyes:

> *Our sin and misery are made an occasion of our greater blessedness.*
>
> *This is a very wonderful thing. It would have been a very wonderful thing if we had been merely restored from sin and misery, to be as we were before, but it was a **much more wonderful** thing that we should be brought to a*

higher blessedness than ever; and that our sin and misery should be the occasion of it, and should make way for it.

(1.) It was wonderful that sin should be made the occasion of our **greater blessedness**, for sin deserves misery. By our sin we had deserved to be everlastingly miserable. But this is so turned by divine wisdom that it is made an occasion of our being **more happy**. It was a strange thing that sin should be the occasion of anything else but misery. But divine wisdom has found out a way whereby the sinner might not only escape being miserable, but that he should be **happier than before he sinned**. Yea, than he would have been if he had never sinned at all. And this sin and unworthiness of his are the occasion of this **greater blessedness**.

(2.) It was a wonderful thing that man's own misery should be an occasion of his **greater happiness**, for happiness and misery are opposites and man's misery was very great. He was under the wrath and curse of God and condemned to everlasting burnings. But the sin and misery of man, by this design, are made an occasion of his being **more happy, not only than he was before the fall, but than he would have been if he never had fallen**. Our first parents, if they had stood and persevered in perfect obedience till God had given them the fruit of the tree of life as a seal of their reward, would probably have been advanced to higher happiness, for they before were but in a state of probation for their reward. And it is not to be supposed but that their happiness was to have been greater after they had persisted in obedience, and had actually received the reward, than it was while they were in a state of trial for it. But by the redemption of Christ, the sin and misery of the elect are made an occasion of their being brought to a **higher happiness** than mankind would have had if they had persisted in obedience till they had received the reward.

For, 1st, man is hereby brought to a **greater and nearer** union with God. If man had never fallen God would have remained man's friend. He would have enjoyed God's favor and so would have been the object of Christ's favor, as he would have had the favor of all the persons of the Trinity. But now Christ becoming our surety

32

*and Savior, and having taken on him our nature, creates between Christ and us a union of a quite different kind, and a **nearer** relation than otherwise would have been. The fall is the occasion of Christ's becoming our head and the church his body.*

*And believers are become his brethren, and spouse, in a manner that otherwise would not have been. And by our union with Christ we have a **greater** union with God the Father. We are sons by virtue of our union with the natural Son of God (Galatians 4:4–6). And therefore Christ has taught us, in all our addresses to God, to call him our Father, in like manner as he calls him Father (John 20:17). This is one of the wonderful things brought about by the work of redemption, that thereby our separation from God, is made an occasion of a **greater** union than was before, or otherwise would have been. When we fell there was a dreadful separation made betwixt God and us. But this is made an occasion of a **greater** union (John 17:20–23).*

*2dly, man now has **greater** manifestations of the glory and love of God, than otherwise he would have had. In the manifestations of these two things, man's happiness principally consists. Now, man by the work of redemption, has **greater** manifestation of both, than otherwise he would have had. We have already spoken particularly of the glory of God, and what advantages even the angels have by the discoveries of it in this work. But if they have such advantages, **much more** will man who is far more directly concerned in this affair than they. Here are immediately **greater** displays of the love of God than man had before he fell, or, as we may well suppose, than he would have had, if he had never fallen. God now manifests his love to his people, by sending his Son into the world, to die for them. There never would have been any such testimony of the love of God, if man had not fallen.*

*Christ manifests his love by coming into the world and laying down his life. This is the **greatest** testimony of divine love that can be conceived. Now surely the **greater** discoveries God' s people have of his love to them, the more occasions will they have to rejoice in that love. Here will be a delightful theme for the saints to contemplate to* all eternity, which they never could have had, if man never had fallen, viz. the dying love of Christ. They will have occasion now to sing that song forever (Revelation 1:5,6).

3rdly, man now has **greater** motives offered him to love God than otherwise he ever would have had. Man's happiness consists in mutual love between God and man, in seeing God's love to him and in reciprocally loving God. And the more he sees of God's love to him, and the more he loves God, the more happy must he be. His love to God is as necessary in order to his happiness as the seeing of God's love to him, for he can have no joy in beholding God's love to him in any otherwise than as he loves God. This makes the saints prize God's love to them, for they love him. If they did not love God, to see his love to them would not make them happy. But the more any person loves another, the more will he be delighted in the manifestations of that other's love. There is provision therefore made for both in the work of redemption. There are **greater** manifestations of the love of God to us, than there would have been if man had not fallen; and also there are **greater** motives to love him than otherwise there would have been. There are **greater** obligations to love him, for God has done more for us to win our love. Christ hath died for us.

Again, man is now brought to a **more** universal and immediate and sensible dependence on God than otherwise he would have been. All his happiness is now of him, through him, in him. If man had not fallen, he would have had all his happiness of God by his own righteousness. But now it is by the righteousness of Christ. He would have had all his holiness of God, but not **so** sensibly, because then he would have been holy from the beginning, as soon as he received his being. But now he is first sinful and totally corrupt, and afterwards is made holy. If man (Adam) had held to his integrity misery would have been a stranger to him, and therefore happiness would not have been **so** sensible a derivation from God, as it is now, when man looks to God from the deeps of distress, cries repeatedly to him, and waits upon him. He is convinced by abundant experience, that he has no place of resort but God, who is graciously pleased, in consequence of man's earnest and persevering prayer, to appear to his relief, to take" him out of the miry clay and horrible pit, set him upon a rock, establish his goings, and put a new song into his mouth." (Ps. 40:1,2) By man's having thus a **more** immediate, universal, and sensible dependence, God doth **more** entirely secure man's undivided respect. There is a **greater** motive for man to make God his all in all, to love him and rejoice in him as his only portion.

4thly, by this design for our salvation man's sin and man's misery are but an occasion of his being brought to a **more** full and free converse with and enjoyment of God than otherwise would have been. For as we have observed already, the union is greater, and the greater the union, the more full the communion and intimate the intercourse. Christ is come down to man in his own nature and hereby he may converse with Christ **more** intimately than the infinite distance of the divine nature would allow. This advantage is **more** than what the angels have. For Christ is not only in a created nature but he is in man's own nature. We have also advantages for a **more** full enjoyment of God. By Christ's incarnation the saints may see God with their bodily eyes as well as by an intellectual view. The saints, after the day of judgment, will consist of both body and soul, that is, they will have outward as well as spiritual sight. It is now ordered by divine wisdom that God himself, or a divine person, should be the principal entertainment of both these kinds of sight, spiritual and corporal. And the saints in heaven shall not only have an intellectual sight of God but they shall see a divine person as they see one another, not only spiritually but outwardly. The body of Jesus Christ will appear with that transcendent visible majesty and beauty, which is exceedingly expressive of the divine majesty, beauty, and glory. The body of Christ shall appear with the glory of God upon it, as Christ tells us. (Thus to see God will be a great happiness to the saints. Job comforted himself that he should see God with his bodily eyes, Job 19:26.)

5thly, man's sin and misery is made an occasion of his **greater** happiness, as he has now a **greater** relish of happiness, by reason of his knowledge of both. In order to be happy there must be two things, viz. union to a proper

35

*object and a relish of the object. Man's misery is made an occasion of increasing both these by the work of redemption. We have shown already that the union is **increased** and so is the relish too, by the knowledge man now has of evil. These contraries, good and evil, heighten the sense of one another. The forbidden tree was called the tree of knowledge of good and evil; of evil because by it we came to the experience of evil; of good, because we should never have known so well what good was, if it had not been for that tree. We are taught the value of good by our knowledge of its contrary, evil. This teaches us to prize good, and makes us the **more** to relish and rejoice in it. The saints know something what a state of sin and alienation from God is. They know something what the anger of God is, and what it is to be in danger of hell. And this makes them the **more exceedingly** to rejoice in the favor and in the enjoyment of God.*

*Take two persons; one who never knew what evil was, but was happy from the first moment of his being, having the favor of God, and numerous tokens of it; another who is in a very sad and undone condition. Let there be bestowed upon these two persons the same blessings, [subjectively,] the same good things; and let them be objectively in the same glorious circumstances. Which one will rejoice **most**? Doubtless he that was brought to this happiness out of a miserable and sorrowful state. So the saints in heaven will forever the **more** rejoice in God and in the enjoyment of his love for their being brought to it out of a most lamentable state and condition."[4]*

I could have answered this third question with a short "No" and moved on to other things, I guess. But don't you want to go back and read Edwards' analysis again and soak it in: that God knew what He was doing all along. The Fall was part of the overall design, not an aberration or unforeseen glitch in His perfect plan. God had created so that He could redeem. He didn't redeem because He had created, as a way of salvaging something from the

---

[4] Jonathan Edwards, *The Works of Jonathan Edwards*, Vol. 2, Section 6, page 150–151.

debris. Without being the author of evil, through creation, He became the conqueror of evil by redemption and righteous judgment (Acts 15:18; Rom. 9:14–33).

Reflections

1. Do you remember the question the Beatles asked in the chorus of "Eleanor Rigby": "All the lonely people, where do they all come from?" How should we answer their question? According to this chapter, there are two answers that explain loneliness as we know it today. Can you state them in your own words?

2. How has sin created and contributed to my personal experience of loneliness? (e.g. parental abuse, cruelty of friends, job related conflict, spousal misconduct)

3. In my own experience do I distinguish between the original, God-intended place of loneliness and the sinful distortion sin has brought into the world? How does my answer affect my attitude towards God? How does my attitude make my loneliness worse or better?

4. If I have heard you correctly...

   ...then I should find other scriptures to support the idea that Adam's fall has altered the original conditions of creation. I have found the following that do lend credence to that idea.

   ...then I should find other scriptures that support the amazing idea that God was not surprised by the fall, but had planned for it from before the creation of the world. I have found the following scriptures that say that:

   ...then God has not abandoned us. Therefore, I should express to Him my praise and thanks, and seek His provision for my loneliness even more than if Adam and Eve had not sinned.

Previews

1. Begin today to keep a journal of your loneliness. Do this to:
   - better understand <u>when</u> you get lonely
   - better understand <u>what</u> seems to trigger it, if anything
   - discern <u>what kinds</u> of feelings accompany or characterize your loneliness
   - begin to store up the resources that help you during lonely times.

2. If Edwards was right, why did God hold Adam and Eve responsible for sin if they were just fulfilling His great design?

3. Is God happy? Does He enjoy what the world became and is?

4. Is God's rule of the universe mediate or immediate? That is, does He directly control all things, like a signalman in a railroad control tower? Or does He indirectly control all things through appointed means, like natural forces, angels, human agency? Or does He control all things at all?

INTERLUDE

IF (FOR AMY)

pts (8-13-02)

if slowly, too slowly, You withered her life
who to me is most like You when traced
if she dangled over death's pit by but a ray of light
how could we face it, except by Your grace
if I take what You give then I'll give what You take

if quickly, too quickly, You snatched her away
with no word of warning, without any delay
how could we face it, except by Your grace
if I take what You give then I'll give what You take

the truth is so plain (now) even I can see
no matter the when's and how's it's too much for me
I cannot fathom the chasm of all that's involved
whether slow or quick
give me Your grace, save me from murmur's spite
all I have, You gave me
You take but Your own

THE MAKING OF POEMS

Gregory Orr

Gregory Orr has taught English at the University of Virginia since 1975. He is the author of nine poetry collections and the recipient of NEA and Guggenheim fellowships. Orr lives in Charlottesville, Va., with his wife, the painter Trisha Orr.

When I was 12 years old, I was responsible for the death of my younger brother in a hunting accident. I held the rifle that killed him. In a single moment, my world changed forever. I felt grief, terror, shame and despair more deeply than I could ever have imagined. In the aftermath, no one in my shattered family could speak to me about my brother's death, and their silence left me alone with all my agonizing emotions. And under those emotions, something even more terrible: a knowledge that all the easy meanings I had lived by until then had been suddenly and utterly abolished.

One consequence of traumatic violence is that it isolates its victims. It can cut us off from other people, cutting us off from their own emotional lives until we go numb and move through the world as if only half alive. As a young person, I found something to set against my growing sense of isolation and numbness: the making of poems.

When I write a poem, I process experience. I take what's inside me—the raw, chaotic material of feeling or memory—and translate it into words and then shape those words into the rhythmical language we call a poem. This process brings me a kind of wild joy. Before I was powerless and passive in the face of my confusion, but now I am active: the powerful shaper of my experience. I am transforming it into a lucid meaning.

Because poems are meanings, even the saddest poem I write is proof that I want to survive. And therefore it represents an affirmation of life in all its complexities and contradictions.

An additional miracle comes to me as the maker of poems: because poems can be shared between poet and audience, they also become a further triumph over human isolation.

Whenever I read a poem that moves me, I know I'm not alone in the world. I feel a connection to the person who wrote it, knowing that he or she has gone through something similar to what I've experienced, or felt something like what I have felt. And their poem gives me hope and courage, because I know that they survived, that their life force was strong enough to turn experience into words and shape it into meaning and then bring it toward me to share. The gift of their poem enters deeply into me and helps me live and believe in living.[5]

---

[5]"The Making of Poems" was aired on NPR's "All Things Considered," February 20, 2006. (The recording and transcript are available online at http://www.npr.org/templates/story/story.php?storyId=5221496)

Part Two:
Sketches of Loneliness

INTRODUCTION TO PART 2

I've never looked at the Bible as a book about lonely people. I think it's wrong to make the Bible something other than what it intends to be—the inspired word of God on His redemptive work. That said, it is nevertheless true that the biblical account contains numerous individuals whose peculiar situations reveal the human condition to our careful consideration (Rom. 15:4; Heb.11:1–12:3). Their ordeal was recorded to help us through ours (Job 19:21–29; Ps.78:1–11). This gracious design on the part of the Author necessitates our diligent digging and application if we are to extract the vital truths that God has embedded there, for our help and comfort (Heb.11:6).

What we are about to embark upon is a collection of sketches of various biblical personalities. I use the word "sketches" intentionally. These will not be portraits, for portraits are detailed and fully colored renditions of scenery or persons. Sketches, on the other hand, are black and white attempts to get a sense of the person or scene. That is what I intend by the upcoming chapters.

There have been moments during this journey into loneliness that I have felt like I am trespassing in someone's private cemetery, or taking a self-guided tour of someone's house or dresser drawer. If you feel that way about this study, if you have thought *"This guy has no idea what he's talking about. He hasn't experienced what I have,"* please forgive my rough handling of such delicate matters. You are correct, of course. I haven't experienced what you have or are experiencing of loneliness. But then, no one has had the exact same experience as anyone else. But that doesn't render them useless to observe and help. May God help us both to come somewhere close to the middle ground, where we are both thinking scripturally and feeling humanly (Prov. 14:10).

CHAPTER 3

AN EMPTY WELL, FILLED

I realize John 4 and Genesis 3 are miles apart in terms of time and Bible landscape, but let's leap across the millennia and see a troubled woman and a tired Savior meeting, much as we saw a troubled Adam and a searching God in the garden of Eden.

The account in John 4 begins with 2 lonely people meeting at a well. Christ Jesus was resting beside Jacob's well, near Sychar, while His disciples went into the village to purchase food (4:5, 6). This was the land of Samaria, a separate entity from Israel, both ethnically and religiously. The Samaritans were traditional antagonists to the Jewish inhabitants of Galilee to the north and Judea to the south. In the Old Testament this area had once been the kingdom of Israel, led by non-Davidic kings and they worshipped many gods other than the one, true God. Ultimately, God had sent most of them into captivity at the hands of the Assyrians, and in their place they brought peoples from their other conquests. The resulting inter-marriages produced a race of people that worshipped a variety of gods, including Jehovah. These people became the Samaritans, so famous in the New Testament times. The continual friction between the Jews and Samaritans is very much like the current tensions between Israelis and Palestinians. So the Lord was doubly alone—left by His disciples in a foreign and hostile country.

The second party in this drama, a woman, was also doubly alone. She came to the well by herself, where Jesus was resting. She was a Samaritan from the nearby village. One wonders if the disciples had passed her on their way in to get food. Although she was a native of that place we soon learn that she was very much a stranger in it, rendering her also doubly alone. This alienation came to the surface when Jesus asked her for a drink of water (4:9). She challenged his request for three reasons: religion, race and gender. Each of these is still a battleground we struggle with each other and ourselves about (4:11,12,19). The cause or source here is her emptiness of the life of God (4:10). The symptom of her alienation or loneliness was her combative, defensive attitude. The vehicle or manner in which this symptom was conveyed was her words. With amazing patience and depth of insight Jesus turned the tables on her, offering to give her a drink (despite those 3 barriers), a drink she needed so desperately.

His manner reminds me of the way God approached Adam in Genesis 2, when He brought him to desire the helpmate which God wanted him to have. Notice, too, how vaguely and yet how pointedly Jesus probed the woman's heart (4:10, 13–15).

How did the unnamed woman respond to this line of conversation? She reacted more positively after Jesus had spoken to her than she had at the outset. She accepted His offer of water that would quench her thirst, even though she didn't know what it all meant (4:15). She could've rejected Him completely at this point and gone on with her business, empty in heart, carrying her full water jug back to her home. But she responded favorably, despite those three barriers—religion, race, and gender.

End of story, right? Wrong. Jesus refused to grant her the refreshing drink He had promised her a few moments before. She knew too little to give her what she needed.

So He suddenly pulled the cup from her lips and knocked the cup from her hands, so to speak. She had to go home first and get her husband and return before He would give her the living water (4:16).

May I ask you a personal question? Did you find yourself struggling with the first two chapters of this study? Did it seem too theoretical, too cold, too remote from what your heart struggles with? Did you sigh and say to yourself, *"This isn't what I need. This guy is just wasting his time and mine. I'm lonely. I don't need to be educated about creation and sin"?* If you did you are probably going to have the same difficulty with the Lord Jesus' behavior in John 4:16–26. Why did He instruct her to leave Him, go get her husband and then return, presumably to receive the thirst quenching drink He had offered her? Why had God asked Adam where he was, after he and Eve had sinned? For the same reason He had made Adam name the animals, namely, to provoke self-reflection, leading to a deep sense of need, so as to come to confess that need and receive God's help. It is exactly the same thing here.

She responded to Christ's evangelistic blunder by denying that she had any husband (4:17). A technically true statement, Jesus agreed (4:18) but also morally false. She had had five husbands in the past and currently was either living with a man outside of marriage or conducting an adulterous affair with a married man. But why bring this up now? What did her marital and moral history have to do with her spiritual thirst, which Jesus had promised to quench forever and to turn her into an artesian spring of inner sufficiency? (4:14)

The first question Jesus had asked had provoked defensive words from her, which had revealed the alienation she felt towards Him over religion, race and gender. Without the probing questions that attitude would not have surfaced and, undetected, would have been beyond remedy. He had probed that He might heal. The same is true here. He probed deeper into her soul because the problem was deeper than she knew or admitted to herself. By forcing her to face the depths of her alienation, her internal dislocation, Christ was lancing a festering, poisonous infection that made any attempt at superficial cures out of the question. No good doctor medicates symptoms and leaves the disease untouched. And Christ is the great Physician!

Her deepest problem was her inner alienation. She had not found a place for God in her lonely soul. Put differently, she had not dealt with designed loneliness well because she had not come to grips with the problem of sin—hers and Adam's. Her designed loneliness—the kind God intended to make us need other humans and be to them what they needed—was unmet and she had spent her adult life trying to make men fill that void, with catastrophic results. Remember, when God made Eve for Adam, it wasn't to take His place in Adam's heart, nor for Adam to take God's place in Eve's heart. They were to be part of God's comprehensive design to fill each other's needs; only a part, not the complete solution. God alone could fill the emptiness that He had created mankind with.

This woman had had five husbands. Even if we allow for several tragic deaths on the part of some of this quintuplet, we can hardly believe all five had died, making her a five-time widow. But even allowing this extreme scenario to have occurred, there is no disputing her current marital status (4:18). She was in a relationship that was immoral by everyone's religious beliefs, and chances are that some of the other marriages had ended due to some other cause than death, such as infidelity, either by the men or by her. This is significant for two reasons.

1. **It pointed out to her the role of sin in making her thirsty, that is, her inner emptiness.**

    As in chapter 2, we must come to grips with both the designed loneliness and the loneliness resulting from personal and Adamic sin. She had to come to the point where she saw just how deep her need was, if she was to receive Christ's help.

    If her husbands had all died, since death came as a result of Adam's sin, she needed to face the connection between spiritual cause and effect in her world.

2. **It brought to light, for her to see, the solutions she had attempted in the past to fill the void.**

    Even if all of her husbands had died, she always returned to a single solution for her loneliness—another husband. Five times she had sought and found, or was sought and was found, by five different men. At present she had altered the formula by not marrying. Can you see the pattern? She didn't, until now, under His cross-examination. The inner drive from the combination of designed and fallen loneliness had led her to find comfort, fulfillment, security, worth and affection in a fallen human being.

48

Each time she was left empty, either by the intrusion of death (tailwaters of the fall) or by his unfaithfulness (tailwaters of the fall again) or by her own unfaithfulness to him (tailwaters of the fall once more). If they had had marital problems those too were the twisted wreckage of Adam's sin, worked out in their own selfishness, anger, laziness or immorality. Each time one marriage ended, her appetite for another man led her to the next candidate—someone more handsome perhaps, more intelligent or more wealthy or more famous or better placed in society or more sensitive. Empty, she was driven, and more empty she left. She was thirsty, but nothing she had tried, including religion, had satisfied her. Our Lord brought her face to face with her own inner Ecclesiastes. "Vanity of vanity, all is vanity," her life cried out.

§

Like Adam and Eve, her ancestors, this woman sought to conceal her true state from God's prying eyes. Not with leaves this time, but with diversions and arguments about religion, one of the three things she had initially used to rebuff Christ's request for water (4:19, 20). I notice that Jesus went up in her estimation from the start of this narrative. From being a distracting, uncouth Jewish beggar (4:9) He had become a mysterious visitor with a magic solution for her thirst (4:15). And now, finally, she viewed Him as a prophet, who knew hidden things intimately. This was by design on His part, as it had been with His procedure with Adam in Genesis 2.

Returning to her rebuttal (4:19,20), notice she had already verbalized this attitude in 4:9, so it was a prominent thought in her mind, which had the effect of making Jesus someone to be held at a distance, someone who wasn't to be trusted or accepted. In short, these words were words of enmity or alienation. We saw this in Adam and Eve in Genesis 3 and later in the murder of Abel by Cain, and finally in the pre-flood violence and immorality (Gen.6:1–12). Christ's direct and clear answer is in contrast to His vague and symbolical answers earlier (4:10–14 compared with 4:21–24, 26). The first type of answer must precede the other, just as a dim light allows the eyes to adjust and accept a brighter light. Instead of debating religion or even returning to her immorality and her vain pursuit of fulfillment in human companionship, Jesus Christ turned her eyes to the future. The future of worship was simple and singular. All will worship the Father, wherever they are (4:21, 22). God had been looking for true worshippers since creation; worshippers who worship Him in spirit and truth, not just in the correct place and through the prescribed ritual (4:23). The reason for such a future and for His present scavenger hunt was due to God's very nature (4:24). Since God is spirit, only spiritual worship, that regards God's revealed truth, can be acceptable to Him.

Overwhelmed? So was she (4:25). She had just come for noonday water and here she was getting a theology lecture from a Jewish prophet. One thing she did know for certain, however. All disagreements about religion and other mysteries will come to an end when God's Messiah, the Christ, comes. Perhaps she meant this as a way of ending the conversation on a pleasant note or she may have sighed these words longingly, hungrily, and thirstily. Christ's answer would indicate the latter explanation to be the more probable one (4:26). He affirmed, absolutely, without veil or parable, that He was that self-same Messiah she thirsted for, and so her expectations could be realized. In fact, she had already experienced His revealing all things! (4:18) This is exactly what drove her in joyful haste back to her village, leaving her water jug behind (4:28).

When she arrived she boldly announced to the men of Sychar that she had met a man that had *"told me all things that I ever did."* (4:29, 39) Was she exaggerating? Had Christ told her everything she had ever done? As far as details, no, but in terms of her life's theme, yes! Coming from *her* to them, *with her background with them*, they knew what this announcement must mean. She posed the question that could have but one answer (4:29). They rushed out to see Him for themselves (4:30).

When the whole affair was finished, two days later, they looked at her and agreed with her final assessment of this Jewish vagrant. He was, indeed, the Messiah. Her discovery was now theirs, on its own merits. She had been the spring that led to quenching their thirst: an empty well, filled. Now, they were springs too. The deserts were now rivers.

Conclusions on Loneliness

Let's summarize some conclusions from this sketch, relative to loneliness.

1. **God seeks lonely, alienated people, to bring them to His overflowing fullness.** To do so is for their good and to His glory.

2. **Human companionship alone is insufficient to satisfy the deep thirst of our souls.** No matter how much or how many we accumulate, no created thing can produce absolute fullness in us. He alone can satisfy the infinite hunger we have. This is for our good and to His glory.

3. **God's methods towards us are always in keeping with the dignity of our original design.** He doesn't deal with us like beasts, plants or rocks, although we may act like them. He approaches us through our reason and conscience, with increasing measures of light, as we respond to the light we have. This is for our good and to His glory.

4. **Christ Jesus is uniquely suited to seek and find lonely people.** He, too, lived in the real world setting, as we do. He, too, experienced humanity after the Fall. Not that He was fallen, but the effects of the Fall, like racism, sectarianism and gender prejudice, were His first-hand experience.

   Being God, Christ brought the great need of man to the light of day, as the means of putting people right in their souls. In other words, when we watched Christ reaching the shattered shards of Adam's posterity we saw Him setting about to put them into a right relationship with God **first**. Then he sent them to fix the brokenness they had encountered with other humans. He brought people back to

God. Then the designed loneliness could once more be a positive force, under God's renewed place of direction.

Being God, He knows everything about us, even that which is hidden from our own eyes (Jer. 17:9,10). He alone can reveal us to ourselves. We can only see ourselves clearly as we see our reflection in His eyes. He must get that close to us.

5. **Our natural tendency is to retreat from the pain truth brings.** We make excuses, find others to blame or engage in diversions and complex speculations. Like Adam and this woman, we are always weaving aprons to cover up the naked truth.

6. **The outcome of this account should both amaze us and fill us with hope.** However much despair and bitterness may be our constant companions, we can be helped and be the means to help others, as we once were the means to harm others. Until she met Christ she was both a cause and a result of alienation and despair in Sychar. His revelation to her of her true condition and His ability to meet her need resulted in her becoming the cause of others' recovery. The wounded make the best healers.

7. **As long as we are completely mindful of our needs only, we will be miserable.** Her greatest need was to become a worshipper, someone oblivious to all else but God, someone who lived to give to Him adoring obedience from her heart, according to His reveled truth. Loneliness is only magnified in front of a mirror. It dwindles before a window, looking out upon the suffering around us. And it is swallowed up when prostrate before the throne.

Reflections

1. Now how would you answer the question, "Does everyone have to have a human companion to be fulfilled?"

2. Is God completely alienated from His creation? Has the sin of Adam and his family forced God to abandon His creation?

3. Does anyone's situation surprise or baffle God? Does He appear to be scrambling for answers or trying to make the best of a bad situation?

4. Do you know anyone like the woman in John 4?

    a. How is he or she similar?

    b. How is he or she different?

    c. Up until now, what have you done for him or her?

    d. What is his or her greatest need? What are the secondary needs?

    e. Which of these can you meet?

f. Did her personal discovery satisfy the men of Sychar? Or was she the means for them finding their own satisfaction in Christ?

5.   If I have heard you correctly . . .

...then I should be able to find other people in scriptures like the woman at the well. So far I have found the following examples in my Bible:

...then loneliness may have a variety of symptoms, not just the ones we normally associate with it. (withdrawal, melancholy, etc.) I might find lonely people who are angry, combative in areas of gender, religion, and race or frequently dating and / or marrying.

...then I should understand that no amount of human companionship will replace the need for divine fullness in the human heart.

Previews

1. Can someone be fulfilled or contented through restored fellowship with God through Christ and have no human companionship of any kind? Is it even possible to live in this world without human assistance of some kind? (Who wrote your Bible? Your favorite song? Who made your instrument?)

2. Is this a female problem? Is it only women who are alone at the well, struggling with loneliness?

3. In what other ways does loneliness manifest itself?

INTERLUDE

THE SOUND AND THE WORRY

Rich Mullins

We are surrounded by—we are dependent on (and weirdly, quite even indebted to) a hundred million things that are just beyond our reach and completely beyond our control; things like favorable weather; the honesty and good intention of those people among whom and with whom we live, work and play; balanced budgets; tomorrow and tomorrow in its creeping, petty pace; our next paycheck; dependable machinery; our next breath.

A hundred million things. All of them are just as real as they are invisible, just as available as they are necessary, just as likely to fall on the just as on the unjust, as apt to shine on those who worry as on those who hope. (The difference being that those who worry are less able to enjoy things than those who hope.) But for all of us, we are surrounded by things we cannot predict, control, possess or avoid—things that press us and compete for control—a competition that must be decidedly won by "faith" or we will be lost.

It is easy in the frantic, task-driven "day-to-day" for us to lose our "centers"—our souls—our sense of who we are and what is really important. We are haunted by the ghosts of the "what-ifs" who live in the shadows of the "if-onlys." They accuse us, torment us, tempt us to abandon the freedom we have in Christ.

But, if we still ourselves, if we let Him calm us, focus us, equip us for the day, He will remind us of our Father's prodigal generosity and about the pitiful weakness of greedy men. He will remind us (as He reminded the devil) that "man does not live by bread alone," though He may call us (as He called His first disciples) to give bread to the hungry (presumably because men cannot live long without bread). He will remind us about the cares that burden common people, the illusions that blind those the world calls "lucky" and the crippling effects of worry. Then He will give us hope—hope that stretches us (where worry bent us) and faith—faith that sustains us (where greed smothered us) and love—love that is at the bottom of our deepest desires, the loss of which is at the root of all our fears.

The other night I dreamt that I was stuck in an airport terminal—another cancelled flight; another long, anxious wait. The place was packed with stranded passengers and misplaced luggage, and I sank into a chair by the phone booths, waiting for the oxygen masks to drop out of the ceilings (it was a dream, remember). Suddenly, I noticed this distressed man, sobbing, pulling his hair out by the handfuls and so I leaned over to ask him what was the matter and if I could help.

"What's wrong, sir?" I asked. He grabbed yet another handful of his hair and sobbed, "I'm afraid I'm going bald!" he said. And so it goes. We are surrounded by a million possibilities, all of which remind us that we are not the "captains of our own fates." As we face these possibilities, let's remember who our Captain is. Let us not be made captives of worry.[6]

---

[6] Rich Mullins, "The Sound and the Worry," *Release,* July/August 1995.

CHAPTER 4

A FULL WELL, EMPTIED

The heart knows its own bitterness,
and a stranger does not share its joy.

—Proverbs 14:10

Even in laughter the heart may sorrow,
and the end of mirth may be grief.

—Proverbs 14:13

Better is a dry morsel with quietness,
than a house full of feasting with strife.

—Proverbs 17:1

If in John 4 we have a short story of an empty well filled, when we come to examine the next cameo, Solomon, we are confronted with the exact opposite. Here we have a massive epic of a full well emptied. Most of the book of Proverbs, all of the Song of Solomon and Ecclesiastes and extended sections of certain Old Testament historical books bear his impress (1 Kings 1–11:43 and 1 Chron. 28:1—2 Chron. 9:31). The well is "full" as to the amount of information about Solomon.

Ironically, that very fullness reveals the appalling tragedy of the emptying of his full life. Therefore, Solomon fits well at this point as a counterbalance or contrast to the woman at the well.

He brings us to consider loneliness from a perspective we may not have thought of seriously otherwise.

First, we must consider the facts. Let's start with the full well.

Solomon's Monarchy: Phase 1

Solomon was a son of King David and Bathsheba (2 Sam. 12:24; 1Kings 1:11). David had many sons and many wives (unfortunately), but Solomon was the offspring from his favorite wife. He was also known as Jedidiah (2Sam. 12:25). *Solomon* means "peace" or "fullness" in Hebrew and *Jedidiah* means "loved of the LORD."

Solomon was chosen to be king by David. Despite his being younger than many of his half-brothers (1Kings 1:17–53). Consider what David did to make Solomon's appointment effective:

- David admonished Solomon to be devoted to God and His laws (1 Chron. 22:6–13).
- David counseled Solomon about matters of immediate importance to him in his new role (1 Kings 2:1f).
- David made Solomon king while he was still young, giving him experience and visibility (1 Kings 3:7; 1Chron. 22:5; 29:1).
- David made extensive, expensive preparations for Solomon to build the temple, organized the administration of the kingdom, arranged the military and gathered popular support for him (1 Chron. 22:1—29:25).

Take a look at the events of the first phase of Solomon's monarchy:

- He began by removing the evil left over from David's regime (1Kings 2:13–46).
- He prayed for wisdom to be an able ruler (1 Kings 3:4–15).
- He made a treaty with Pharaoh and Egypt, sealing the pact by marrying his daughter (1 Kings 3:1).

- At this stage he loved the Lord and walked obediently in His laws and in the counsel of his dad, but not without some looseness (1 Kings 3:2).

In this first phase of his reign, Solomon prospered incredibly (1 Kings 4:26–34; 10:1–29). In addition to personal prosperity, he also prospered in the areas of national and local organization, national prosperity and peace (1 Kings 4:20–25; 5:4), international fame and acclaim (1 Kings 4:29–34; 10:1f), and literary accomplishments (Proverbs, Ecclesiastes, Song of Solomon).

During this time he engaged in numerous building projects. He successfully constructed the great Temple in 7 years (1 Kings 5:1f—6:38). His personal palace took 13 years to build (1 Kings 7:1). In addition to these two massive accomplishments, he also built:

- the House of the Forest of Lebanon (1 Kings 7:2)
- the Hall of Pillars (1 Kings 7:6)
- the Hall of Judgment (1 Kings 7:7)
- the palace court (1 Kings 7:8)
- the palace for his wife, Pharaoh's daughter (1 Kings 7:8)
- the 2 bronze pillars, Jachin and Boaz (1 Kings 7:15–22)
- the bronze sea and oxen for the temple (1 Kings 23–26)
- the temple carts and wash basins (1 Kings 7:27–39)
- miscellaneous projects (1 Kings 9:15–28; 10:12f)

Whew! Exactly. But before you jump to the wrong conclusion about Solomon's prosperity please read Deuteronomy 17:14f and 1 Samuel 8:10f. Do you see what I see? Unmixed prosperity is not an unmixed blessing. The dark side of Solomon's life is only appreciable against this dazzling background.

Next we see the full well, emptied.

Solomon's Monarchy: Phase 2

Solomon's tragedy was that he loved wrongly. He loved too many women. He loved the wrong women. And he loved them too well (1 Kings 11:1f; Neh. 13:26). God had warned through Moses that multiplying wives was dangerous because they would turn the control center—the heart—away from God. Once the steering faculty of the soul was out of God's control, nothing else would be acceptable or right.

Solomon proved God right. In the end, when Solomon was old, those whom he had gathered to display his greatness and secure his country against war and indulge his appetites were the cause of his fall from greatness, bringing ceaseless wars and alienation of his affections from all the excess (1 Kings 11:2–8).

Consider the consequences of Solomon's collapse (1 Kings 11:9–43):

- He was rejected by the righteous God who had blessed him so (11:9–13).
- He was preserved by the faithfulness and mercy of God (11:12).

Consequently, he experienced **the following chastisements** from God:

- Hadad the Edomite, supported by Pharaoh, led a guerilla war in the south (11:14–22).
- Rezon, a Syrian, led a similar insurgency from Damascus in the north (11:23–25).
- Jeroboam ben Nebat, a Jew and former servant of Solomon, was chosen by God to receive part of the empire after Solomon's death. He fled from the vengeful king to Pharaoh in Egypt, and later fulfilled the prophecy by leading a revolt against Solomon's son, Rehoboam (11:26–40).

Taken all together, Solomon's positive accomplishments were effectively eroded before he died in 931 B.C. and continued to decay for the remainder of the history of the nation. All he had gathered, built, organized, lectured about and negotiated unraveled because he loved wrongly. Due to his high and influential position, his decisions for good or ill had international repercussions. Therefore, like Adam, because he chose wrongly countless others felt the ripple effect.

Before we analyze how all this relates to loneliness, let me strongly recommend that the reader pause at this point and take some time to read Solomon's own account of his life, contained in the profoundly penetrating book of Ecclesiastes. In preparation for this chapter I read all of Solomon's writings and carefully thought of his words in the light of how he lived. In many instances in the Proverbs it seems that he was telling his children to do as he said and not as he did. Or it may be he wrote those things before his fall, late in life. In either event, reading Proverbs and knowing the human author is quite a sobering experience in the need for persevering holiness.

But when I read Ecclesiastes I came to understand the dynamic that led to Solomon's downfall. That's why I recommend that the reader go to that book, because it is the best explanation for how such a downfall happened to such a man as he was.

I will permit myself one general observation from Ecclesiastes that is pivotal for what is to follow here. Whatever Solomon became later in life was the direct result of his scientific attempt to solve the mystery of contentment in a fallen world. Solomon did all that he did intentionally, conducting experiments upon himself to find what one thing could fill the void everyone has in them (1:12–2:26). It was in pursuit of finding a cure for the double-barreled loneliness that drives the world that Solomon inflicted upon himself, like Dr. Jekyll, an experiment that destroyed him and countless others.

The woman at the well probably fell into her life's woes accidentally or haphazardly. But the son of David pre-meditated, researched, observed, and wrote down his plan like a 20th-century behavioral scientist.

Contrast this with St. Augustine's testimony of his experience, at the age of 16, with the passionate pursuit of passion:

"I wish now to review in memory my past wickedness
and the carnal corruptions of my soul—not because I still
love them, but that I may love thee, O my God. For love of

thy love I do this, recalling in the bitterness of self-examination my wicked ways, that thou mayest grow sweet to me, thou sweetness without deception! Thou sweetness happy and assured! Thus thou mayest gather me up out of those fragments in which I was torn to pieces, while I turned away from thee, O Unity, and lost myself among "the many." For as I became a youth, I longed to be satisfied with worldly things, and I dared to grow wild in a succession of various and shadowy loves. My form wasted away, and I became corrupt in thy eyes, yet I was still pleasing to my own eyes—and eager to please the eyes of men.

But what was it that delighted me save to love and to be loved? Still I did not keep the moderate way of the love of mind to mind—the bright path of friendship. Instead, the mists of passion steamed up out of the muddy concupiscence of the flesh, and the hot imagination of puberty, and they so obscured and overcast my heart that I was unable to distinguish pure affection from unholy desire. Both boiled confusedly within me, and dragged my unstable youth down over the cliffs of unchaste desires and plunged me into a gulf of infamy. Thy anger had come upon me, and I knew it not. I had been deafened by the clanking of the chains of my mortality, the punishment for my soul's pride, and I wandered farther from thee, and thou didst permit me to do so. I was tossed to and fro, and wasted, and poured out, and I boiled over in my fornications—and yet thou didst hold thy peace, O my tardy Joy! Thou didst still hold thy peace, and I wandered still farther from thee into more and yet more barren fields of sorrow, in proud dejection and restless lassitude.

If only there had been someone to regulate my disorder and turn to my profit the fleeting beauties of the things around me, and to fix a bound to their sweetness, so that the tides of my youth might have spent themselves upon the shore of marriage! Then they might have been tranquilized and satisfied with having children, as thy law prescribes, O Lord—O thou who dost form the offspring of our death and art able also with a tender hand to blunt the thorns which were excluded from thy paradise! For thy omnipotence is not far from us even when we are far from thee. Now, on the other hand, I might have given more vigilant heed to the voice from the clouds: "Nevertheless, such shall have trouble in the flesh, but I spare you," and, "It is good for a man not to touch a woman," *and,* "He that is unmarried cares for the things that belong to the Lord, how he may please the Lord; but he that is married cares for the things that are of the world, how he may please his wife." *I should have listened more attentively to these words, and, thus having been* "made a eunuch for the Kingdom of Heaven's sake," *I would have with greater happiness expected thy embraces.*

But, fool that I was, I foamed in my wickedness as the sea and, forsaking thee, followed the rushing of my own tide, and burst out of all thy bounds. But I did not escape thy scourges. For what mortal can do so? Thou wast always by me, mercifully angry and flavoring all my unlawful pleasures with bitter discontent, in order that I might seek pleasures free from discontent. But where could I find such pleasure save in thee, O Lord—save in thee, who dost teach us by sorrow, who wounds us to heal us, and kills us that we may not die apart from thee. Where was I, and how far was I exiled from the delights of thy house, in that sixteenth year of the age of my flesh, when the madness of lust held full sway in me—that madness which grants indulgence to human shamelessness, even though it is forbidden by thy laws—and I gave myself entirely to it."[7]

Conclusions on Loneliness

1. Solomon's life reveals a side of loneliness that has similarities to Adam's story.

Both had *incredible* assets to start out with, and yet both squandered their riches and those of their posterity by pursuing what God had forbidden. Both, taken together, put to death the lie that prosperity is the cure for loneliness. Those who have

---

[7] St. Augustine, *The Confessions of St. Augustine, Book 2.*
(See the Appendix for more from Augustine on this subject.)

abundance of material goods, intellectual attainments or human companions are no more likely to be content and satisfied with that wealth than those in the exact opposite condition—alone on a desert island.

2. **Solomon's approach to solving the riddle of life's meaning should find a ready audience in our pseudo-scientific society.**

    Unlike the woman in John 4 he cold-bloodedly, methodically, systematically pursued satisfaction, but with no lasting personal success. He was not driven by the same natural things that Adam and the John 4 woman were—physical companionship and security. He was surrounded by more male and female companions than he should have been, both from rational considerations and from divine revelation. Instead, Solomon seemed to subordinate all other concerns, including God, to his one supreme drive—**to know**, categorically and comprehensively. Doesn't that sound like what Satan offered Eve?

    The manifestations of Solomon's loneliness or emptiness were as follows:

    - An unrelenting restlessness—like the devil (1Peter 5:8; Job 1:7,2:2) Solomon pursued his quarry. We see such people as workaholics or ambitious or purpose driven, but in Solomon's case it was a reflection of discontentedness, combined with an insatiable mental curiosity.
    - An unrelenting tendency towards grandeur or splendor, as opposed to looking for simplicity and striving for less.
    - A blindness to the self-application of his own wisdom, God's gift to him. It's difficult for me, at times, to forget that the same fellow who wrote such good counsel (Proverbs 17:1) was so terrible at practicing what he preached.

    From this we should expand our view of loneliness to include some of those people who attempt to fill the contentment void by shopping, collecting, micro-managing their own life or the lives of others, travel incessantly or have a burgeoning social life. They may be dealing with the pangs of loneliness rather than living the good life we imagined they had.

3. The legacy of Solomon's life is primarily negative.

His positive contributions are his written works and his own example. His example serves as a shocking model of what to avoid. He is one of those people whose end always taints the rest of their life's history, like Judas Iscariot or Samson or Saul. In Solomon's case he was and is responsible for the following:

- The division of the nation after his death.

- Wars with surrounding kingdoms and within his own kingdom, which took unnumbered lives and caused nameless sorrow and loneliness on the part of widows, orphans and other family members.

- Sowing the seeds (idolatry and rebellion towards God) which led to a harvest of national exile from which Israel has yet to recover.

- Unknown emotional pain and anger, with their consequent actions, on the part of a thousand women. Even his original wife had to have suffered because of her husbands 999 affairs! What would Jesus have said if He had met Solomon at the well instead of that woman?

4. How shall we explain Solomon?

Can we blame his upbringing? His education? His society? His DNA? His economic situation? His friends? God? Rather than affixing blame I prefer to let Solomon be a mirror that I may look into to see myself by. While all of the aforementioned items may have their part in contributing to Solomon's tragedy the key matter for us is what he was at heart, what we all are at heart: empty, hungry, thirsty. We are that by design, which God meant to bring us to Him, and we are that due to sin—ours and our fellow travelers'. Sin–caused emptiness is intended by God to bring us to Him, too (John 4; Eccl. 2:24–26, 3:9–22).

5. Since contentment has entered into our discussion of loneliness again, we should examine this concept very carefully.

Read Philippians 4:10–13, 1 Tim. 6:3–12, Eccl. 5:10–6:9 carefully and notice how well they harmonize. Realize that the last passage, Ecclesiastes 5:10f, was Solomon's own conclusion from his educational process, just as Paul "*had learned*" from his life of hard knocks.

This topic is too vast to detail here but permit me to make one observation relative to Solomon's statement on contentment. It is found in 5:18–6:2. He learned that any amount of gain without an accompanying ability from God to enjoy that gain only multiplies the emptiness within. God holds the keys to our inner fulfillment and He can unlock our inner vault and fill us up apart from our possessions or companions or with them. But if He withholds the gift of the ability to enjoy the created things in their proper place, we will not have joy but bitter vanity for our sacrifices and mad pursuits (Proverbs 2:20, 30:7–9, 15, 16).

6. Solomon also counsels us about human companionship itself (Eccl. 4:7–12).

Relatively speaking friendships, partnerships and marriage have advantages over solitude. The solution for Adam, Solomon, and the woman of John 4 was not celibacy or monasticism but the correct relationship with other humans, according to God's ordained will. In some instances God wants some individuals to forego marriage and other companionships for His own purposes (1 Cor. 7:8,17, 29–37; Matt. 19:10–12).

We will look at this in a future chapter. It is enough for now to take Solomon's counsel, under the Holy Spirit's inspiring ministry, and learn these two vital lessons:

1. In a fallen world, it's good to have friends we can aid and who can aid us in our struggles (2 Cor. 1:3–11; Eccl. 4:7–12).
2. In a fallen world, no human friendship can replace God Himself in our hearts. (Eccl. 3:10–15; 2 Tim. 4:16–18)

Solomon's abuse of a good thing—marriage or building projects or business—does not invalidate all marriages, all building projects or all business ventures. To retreat to celibacy or hermit-like-living would be equally an abuse of God's ordained plan and result in as much if not more trouble than its opposite.

Reflections

1. Do you know someone like Solomon? What can you do for them?

2. Are they intentionally and continually experimenting with their life, like a lab rat, or is their incessant pursuit more random and haphazard? Did you ever realize they are trying to fill the void?

3. How does Solomon's life comment on the world we live in today? What drives the great majority of people and almost all of the businesses of our world?

4. If I take Solomon and the woman in John 4 to heart and consideration I will embrace the following practices or attitudes or thinking as my own.

5. What other Scriptures can you list that support the insights found in this chapter?

INTERLUDE

FROM AN INTERVIEW WITH RICH MULLINS

I would always be frustrated with all those relationships even when I was engaged. I had a ten-year thing with this girl and I would often wonder why, even in those most intimate moments of our relationship, I would still feel really lonely. And it was just a few years ago that I finally realized that friendship is not a remedy for loneliness. Loneliness is a part of our experience and if we are looking for relief from loneliness in friendship, we are only going to frustrate the friendship. Friendship, camaraderie, intimacy, all those things, and loneliness live together in the same experience.

When I wrote <u>Doubly Good To You</u>, we were getting married, and I had written that for our wedding. A friend of mine said, "Boy that is a really cruel song." And I said, "Well, why?" and she said, "Because you are inferring that if God doesn't give you a love that is centered around someone that is true that he hasn't been doubly good to you. I'm like, "Well, exactly." But God doesn't have to be singly good to anybody. We all have got it better than we deserve so we should be thankful for what we have.[8]

---

[8] Taken from the script of a radio broadcast of "20 The Countdown Magazine Pays Tribute to Rich Mullins," October 11, 1997. (Full script

SERMON ON REVELATION 3:20

Jonathan Edwards

Consider this, that the happiness of men consists in union and friendship with some other being. The Creator alone can be fully happy in the enjoyment of himself. The creature has not enough in himself to fill his own desires, and the heart seeks some other being to be happy in. Man is a creature who cannot be happy but in union and friendship. If he alone is united to none as his friend, he is desolate.

Now when shall we ever have a better offer? When shall we have the offer of a more glorious friendship to be united to than the offer to be united to the person of the Son of God? A life of love to Christ and communion with Christ is the most happy life of all.[9]

can be read at http://kidbrothers.net/words/interviews/20-the-countdown-magazine-oct1197.html)

[9] Sermon preached to the Indians at Stockbridge February 1751. Published in *Works of Jonathan Edwards: Sermons and Discourses 1743-1758*, 25:740.

CHAPTER 5

LONE RANGERS

As we scan the scriptures for counsel about loneliness and its relatives, our minds repeatedly meet certain individuals whose lives are often put on display for all eyes to gaze at. They were set apart by God to be His *watchmen* (Isa. 62:6, 7), His mouthpieces, His very embodiment (Hosea 1–3). They were the prophets. Among the writing prophets two are outstanding in the area in which we are interested. They were contemporaries, although we don't know if they knew each other. They lived at the end of the history of Judah, in the last part of the 7th century before Christ and into the 6th century before Christ. I am speaking about Jeremiah ben Hilkiah from Anathoth, in Benjamin, and Ezekiel ben Buzi, who wrote in captivity in Babylon, by the Chebar river. Following our cameo format we will consider them separately, beginning with Jeremiah, and then summarize them together at the end.

Jeremiah

Jeremiah's loneliness is probably the most extreme case of loneliness of anyone in Scripture, excluding the Lord Jesus Christ. To justify that claim and to understand new facets about loneliness, examine the following evidence with me.

First, Jeremiah's life was "interrupted" by His Creator when he was just "*a youth.*" (Jer. 1:4–6) God asserted His absolute rights over Jeremiah's life by commissioning him to the prophetic ministry at a time when such ministries were not

71

welcome and short lived. Nevertheless God summoned him to His service, based on His prerogatives as Creator and according to His divine designs (1:5).

Second, despite Jeremiah's objection that he was too young (1:6) God persisted in His assertions (1:7). No limitations or obstacles or opposition would dissuade Him from that which He had formulated before time. Jeremiah's insufficiency would be compensated for by God's all sufficiency (1:7–9). God gave him the coordinates for his ministry and the contents of his message and then He confronted the monster that lurked in the shadows behind the prophet's excuses—*fear* (1:8). He was not **sending** a boy into the battle. He was **leading** him into it, keeping him company as together they marched into danger (1:9,10).

Why do I describe the mission of Jeremiah in such gloomy terms? Isn't ministry a glamorous, popular and fulfilling occupation? We don't have time to answer that directly, but the reason I describe God's call upon Jeremiah so darkly is because God did (1:8,10–19). He told Jeremiah exactly what lay before him, as a prophet sent to such people as Judah was at that time. Jeremiah was to be the bearer of bad news to an obstinate, sin-addicted nation, and God mercifully revealed to him that their response to him would be negative (1:19).

The ensuing chapters of Jeremiah prove God to be a reliable witness. Jeremiah obediently proclaimed God's truth to Judah, in an attempt to turn them from the sin God said must result in judgment. And just as God said, Jeremiah was not welcomed by his hearers. On the contrary, he was treated most wickedly. In 11:18–23 Jeremiah learned from God that his hometown was plotting to kill him. Anathoth was a village of priests, whose lives revolved around the sanctuary of God in Jerusalem, just a few miles to the south. But that sacred privilege did not keep them from premeditating the murder of one of their relatives and townsmen.

When Jeremiah heard this news he fell into a bitterly honest prayer to God about His management of life (12:1–4). God's wisdom, justice or righteousness and goodness were all in question to Jeremiah's mind, given what he had found out about the men of Anathoth. He hadn't received any support form his hometown or his fellow priests. How can he expect any from the other towns in Judah? He was alone.

God replied to Jeremiah's prayer in 12:5, 6. Jeremiah only knew part of the bad news. The rest was even worse. His own family was in on the plot to kill him. They were actually setting him up by their false affection and words. Jeremiah was more alone than even he knew. If the news of his town's murderous plot had overwhelmed him, how could he withstand the news that his own brothers and parents were in on that plot? His loneliness is compounded.

Following this heartbreaking disclosure God comforts Jeremiah by telling him of His own heartbreak, received by the betrayal of His people for the gods of the nations (12:7–17). The only companion Jeremiah has in his ordeal, who can truly and thoroughly hurt with him and help him is God. The prophet, God's mouthpiece, will speak with the same sense of betrayal as God, the sender. They shared the feeling.

Despite their shared heartache, God and Jeremiah had some difficult times together. In 14:19–15:18 Jeremiah wrestled with God over His refusal to call off a drought that He was using to chastise Judah. The Lord, for His part, patiently but clearly explained to Jeremiah what His will is, but the poor man continued to try to twist God's omnipotent arm. In 15:15–18 he itemized what serving God had cost him. He had been persecuted, rebuked, socially separated from his mockers, lived in isolation from normal civic interaction, and suffered pain and misery. At last he is even alienated from his one Companion (15:18).

Far from being apologetic or tenderized God responded by requiring new, more demanding sacrifices from Jeremiah, if he was to continue as His spokesman (16:1–18). These additional rules would have the effect of further alienating Jeremiah from the society of his fellow man. Notice especially that God prohibited him from marrying (16:2) as a mercy to him, so as to spare him the heartache that the coming tribulations would bring upon everyone living in the path of God's wrath (16:3, 4). Feasting and funeral observances were also forbidden to Jeremiah (16:5–8).

Have you added all this up? His hometown and family are violently against him, along with the entire nation of Judah. He can't marry and have a family. He can't let his hair down at cookouts or show his grief at funerals. It doesn't appear to me that Jeremiah had any friends or family to console him. But such an assessment is incorrect. He did have God's fellowship, and we also learn from 32:12–15, 36:4–32 and 45:1–5 that God gave him a human helper, Baruch ben Neriah. He seems to have been Jeremiah's secretary and he also had legal standing in the community. We can't tell how friendly they were but we can safely say that Baruch was with Jeremiah in his most difficult times, even when he was kidnapped and taken to Egypt (43:3).

This all adds up to the following conclusion: Jeremiah was called by God to a most hostile life, of long duration, with little human companionship. I have only summarized the compelling details that are found in the book of Jeremiah. If the reader will read it carefully he or she will be confirmed in the conclusions that I have just made.

Jeremiah also authored another book in the Old Testament. Lamentations contains the profound observations of Jeremiah at the fall of Jerusalem, which he witnessed in 586 B.C. Its very name in English describes its sorrowful theme. Chapter 3 contains Jeremiah's own personal lamentation for his life's course. As you read this please note the degree of his sufferings (3:1–18) and then how he did not succumb to despair or bitterness for his hard life (3:19–66). What activities did he engage in to keep from falling headlong into the pit of despondency? (3:19–45)

The Lord Jesus Christ was once asked about divorce and remarriage (Matt. 19:3–9). His response was so provocative that his disciples concluded that if Jesus was right it would be better not to marry than to be so tightly bound to your marriage partner (Matt. 19:10). Christ's reply to them was not to deny their conclusion but to make them aware that **"not everyone can accept"** such a narrow way of life as marriage really is (Matt. 19:11). He then identified 3 groups of **"eunuchs"** to whom it was **"given"** to live apart from the marriage companionship:

1. A providentially or genetically caused temperament which makes one able to live alone. (Matt. 19:12)
2. Man-made or involuntary celibacy. In the Old Testament we read of officials of court who had been forced to become eunuchs in order to serve in the positions they were in (see Matt. 19:12; Esther 2:3–9; Dan. 1:3–11).
3. Self-made or voluntary celibacy. Some individuals give the kingdom of heaven such a level of value that marriage would compete with this dedication. So they give up the right of marriage for the privilege of serving the greater cause (Matt. 19:12 1Cor. 7:1–7, 17–24, 29–35).

Which of these 3 categories best fits Jeremiah's experience? Did he seem to hunger for companionship or was he unaffected by his isolation? If God was the One who chose this path for him and enforced it more and more stringently over the course of Jeremiah's life what does that reveal about God? About man in God's world? About the role of human companionships?

Ezekiel

In harmony with Jeremiah's sovereign call by God we find Ezekiel, too, was initiated into the ministry with no uncertain ideas about who was boss. He, too, had his life plans interrupted and set upon a course he otherwise wouldn't have pursued (1:1– 2:3). Ezekiel was already experiencing the results of the sin Jeremiah had preached against for many years. He was *in* the captivity that was God's ultimate solution for rebellion. In Babylon, along with thousands of others, Ezekiel ben Buzi saw his dreams of becoming a priest in the temple at Jerusalem go up in smoke. While Daniel and his three companions found a niche in the palace of Nebuchadnezzar, Ezekiel lived by the Chebar canal, and it was there one day that God majestically and mightily asserted His rights over his creature. In one of the Bible's most exceptional and dramatic entrances, God summoned Ezekiel to be His prophet to the exiles, just as He had chosen Jeremiah to be His prophet to the people still in Judah. Like Jeremiah, Ezekiel was forewarned about the way his ministry would be received (2:4–8; 3:4–11; 3:24–27). Both were sent to be rejected by the rebellious children of Abraham. Both men were Levites by ancestry. Like Jeremiah, Ezekiel was made to minister in some very unusual ways, to convey God's message to his countrymen:

- Ezekiel had his ability to speak taken away, except when speaking God's word. (3:23–27; 33:22)
- Ezekiel was made to act out or dramatize many of God's messages. (4:1–17; 5:1–5; 6:11–14; 12:1–18; 21:18f) No one, in all of the Bible, had a more exotic ministry than Ezekiel!
- Ezekiel had episodes of a trance-like nature in public, by God's design. (8:1–11:25)
- Ezekiel resisted political correctness, speaking the truth boldly to the leaders. (20:1f)

But unlike Jeremiah, Ezekiel was married, either before he was called to the ministry or during his ministry (24:15–24). God called her "*the desire of your eyes*", speaking to Ezekiel (24:16) and given how exotic and eccentric Ezekiel was, she may have been his only intimate friend as well as his wife. Despite this concession, which had been withheld from Jeremiah, Ezekiel's companion became the last and most dramatic of his sermon illustrations. God informed Ezekiel one day that He was going to suddenly take the life of his wife and when it happened Ezekiel was to preach without any interruption or show of sorrow (24:16–17). Good to His word, she did die. 24:18 leads me to believe that she died the next evening after God warned the prophet. He had faithfully preached that morning. She died that evening. And Ezekiel went out the next morning and acted like nothing had happened.

This was so overwhelmingly compelling to the people that for the first and only time in the book we are told that they responded to Ezekiel (24:19). God empowered him to speak a message to their pricked hearts which hammered home to them what hard-heartedness looked like and why it was so unnatural for true lovers to act that way, whether they are human lovers or lovers of God. When the bad news of the destruction of Jerusalem reached their ears, Ezekiel said, they would react just as he had that day. He was a *sig*nificant man: a man whose actions were signs of things to come (24:24).

Can we even begin to understand the cost Ezekiel paid for such small returns? Is it better to be a Jeremiah or an Ezekiel? To have "loved and lost than to never have loved at all"? Who can say?

While they each had some degree of human companionship given to them in their extremities, by God's condescending mercy, they had a greater companion in the Lord who called them in the first place. In each of their circumstances we can see the unparalleled exaltedness of the Creator and Sustainer, from their initial callings throughout their lives. They had Him who is irreplaceable in His proper position as absolute Lord and they had creature support, however few or limited they may have been. And they survived scandal, years of war, persecution, captivity, social rejection and internal civil war.

Conclusions on Loneliness

What can Jeremiah and Ezekiel teach us about loneliness? What strength or insight can we gain from knowing them?

1. As with Adam, God's character is revealed in these accounts.

Without apology or compromise He entered into the conscious realm of two very different men, who lived as contemporaries on opposite ends of the same regional and national catastrophe. In both cases God acted like God, which means He didn't act at all. He simply was Himself. They existed for His purposes —to reveal Himself. He did not exist for their purposes.

2. God enabled them to face the ordeal of their lives with little or no human support.

God enabled them to endure by establishing a close relationship between Himself and the two men in majesty and overwhelming reverence and authority. He sent them intentionally, knowingly into lives of rejection, hostility, spousal death and celibacy, meeting their need for companionship Himself, without intermediary. This is not to trivialize or demean their sufferings during their lives. I'm just trying to explain how they survived their lives.

3. Having God for a partner did not prevent them from suffering loss and loneliness.

This is especially apparent in the case of Jeremiah. In fact, most of their afflictions were directly caused by their complying with God's will for their lives.

4. The only adequate way to resolve the tension that #3 creates in our minds about God's goodness, justice, wisdom, love, etc., is to embrace fully the reality of eternity.

Only if these two men live forever and live better because of their sacrifices can God be exonerated from libel and blame. Their loneliness—in celibacy or loss of spouse; as two unpopular prophets; as exiles among men—forces the issue of time's importance vs. eternity's importance (Rom. 8:18–24; 2Cor.4:16–18). It is only as eternity is put on the scale opposite the wounds of time that they are lightened and shown to be valuable. But if there is no eternity, no resurrection, no judgment in righteousness, the sufferings of time are heavier, exponentially, and too heavy to bear. This holds true for the wrath of God that awaits the unbelieving. Only if their fate is eternally appalling can God's "wasting" of human messengers be justified. God is completely committed to the fact of eternity, and His actions in time show this best.

5. **Neither prophet became the victim of his circumstances.**

The pangs of loneliness, while very real, are not uncontrollable and should not be in control of our lives. They struggled, yes. But they struggled falling forward.

6. **The ways we experience human companionship are more varied than just marriage or friendship.**

In these two cases I see companionship expressed or withheld by the family unit, a hometown population, civic and national leaders, servants and national populations. Each, in their own way, provides some measure of our need for a sense of belonging, not to the exclusion of a mate or close friendships, but as supplements to them. There are a variety of ways our hunger for companionship should be and can be addressed. All of them together cannot render me immune to loneliness. That's the lesson of Solomon. Nor can any one of them being absent condemn me to bondage to loneliness. That's the lesson of Jeremiah and Ezekiel.

INTERLUDE

OF FRIENDSHIP

Francis Bacon

But little do men perceive what solitude is, and how far it extends; for a crowd is not company, and faces are but a gallery of pictures, and talk but a tinkling cymbal where there is no love. The Latin adage addresses it a little, "even in a great town friends are scattered," so that there is not that fellowship, for the most part, which is in less neighborhoods. But we may go further and affirm most truly, that it is a mere and miserable solitude to lack true friends, without which the world is but a wilderness. And even in this sense also of solitude, whosoever in the frame of his nature and affections is unfit for friendship, he takes it of the beast, and not from humanity.[10]

THOUGHTS ON SOLITUDE

Timothy Rogers

See the reason why people in trouble love solitariness. They are full of sorrow. And sorrow, if it has taken deep root, is naturally reserved, and excludes all conversation. Grief is a thing that is very silent and private. Those people that are very talkative and clamorous in their sorrows are never very sorrowful. Some are

---

[10] Francis Bacon, *Essays of Francis Bacon,* "Essay 27: Of Friendship."

apt to wonder, why melancholy people delight to be so much alone, and I will tell you the reason of it.

1. Because the disordered humors of their bodies change their temper, their humors, and their inclinations, that they are no more the same that they used to be. Their very distemper is averse to what is joyous and diverting and they that wonder at them may as wisely wonder why they desire to be diseased, which they would not be if the knew how to help it. But the disease of melancholy is so obstinate and so unknown to all but those who have it, that nothing but the power of God can totally overthrow it, and I know no other cure for it.

2. Another reason why they choose to be alone is because people do not generally mind what they say, nor believe them, but rather deride them, which they do not usually do with those that are in other diseases. And no man is to be blamed for avoiding society when it does not afford the common credit to his words that is due to the rest of men.

3. Another, and the principal reason why people in trouble and sadness choose to be alone is because they generally perceive themselves singled out to be the marks of God's peculiar displeasure, and they are often, by their sharp afflictions, a terror to themselves and a wonder to others. It even breaks their hearts to see how low they are fallen, how oppressed, that were once as easy, as pleasant, as full of hope as others are (Job 6:21; Ps 71:7). And it is usually unpleasant to others to be with them (Ps 88:18). And was it not so with the friends of Job, to see a man whom they had once known happy, to be so miserable; one whom they had seen so very prosperous, to be so very poor, in such sorry, forlorn circumstances? It did greatly affect them. He, poor man, was changed. They knew him not, Job 2:12–13. The prophet speaks of one under spiritual and great afflictions as being one "that sitteth alone, and keepeth silence" (Lam 3:28).[11]

---

[11] Timothy Rogers, *A Discourse on Trouble of Mind, and the Disease of Melancholy,* (Maxwell and Wilson, 1808).

CHAPTER 6

MOSES: ALONE IN A CROWD

In my regular reading through God's Word today I came across the account of Moses and the newly constituted nation of Israel in the Old Testament book of Numbers. Nearly a year or so had elapsed since God rocked the world by extracting slaves out the jaws of that lion of a nation, Egypt. This powerful, merciful, gracious act declared Israel to be a holy nation to God, and with unparalleled favor He granted them detailed laws by which to run every facet of their lives; miraculous provisions with which to sustain their lives; and a priesthood and sanctuary around which to center their spiritual lives (Deut. 4:7, 8; Ps. 147:19, 20).

By the time you get to Numbers 11 you find the nation on the verge of actually enjoying the promises of God in Canaan. Moses, the man of God had used in all of His miraculous and providential displays towards His people, has repeatedly intervened on their behalf with God. This was due to their frequent and flagrant rebellion against the very God who had rescued them and guided them to their present location in the wilderness. But despite all of God's goodness and all of Moses' faithfulness their carnal appetite and insulting unbelief towards God resulted in His righteous anger (11:1). As before, the people looked to Moses to stop God from destroying them, which he did by intercessory prayer (11:2), but not before an unknown number were burned up by God's fire (11:3).

The smoke was still hanging in the air when some of the people just spared began to complain about the food supply, or the lack thereof, and the lack of selection in what food they had.

Compared with the food they had in slavery the present entrees were disgusting, despite being miraculous (11:4–6).

I have reconstructed this scene in order to better appreciate what happened next (11:10–15). It is one of the most transparently melancholy prayers in the Bible, made all the more so by coming from such a man as Moses, with his history of unique spiritual privilege and power. His words only underscore two profound truths:

1. No one is immune to despair
2. One can be very much alone in a crowd

Let's consider the complaint of Moses (Num. 11:10–15) and God's response (Num. 11:16–17).

Moses' Complaint (Num. 11:1015)

The Cause (v. 10)

Moses reacted to the weeping, complaining, unbelieving people with *"displeasure"* (NKJV). Their displeasure spawned his displeasure.

It also seems that Moses' reaction was due to his perception that God's wrath had returned, aggravated and multiplied because of the new offense so soon after He had spared them from another time of chastisement (11:10).

Moses' Reaction (vv. 11–15)

Moses' reaction was directed **at God,** not at the people (11:11–15). As before (11:2) Moses was placed into the role of mediator between sinners and the righteous Judge. However this time Moses manifested a griping, angry attitude towards God. He didn't so much pray for the people as he did for himself. Moses was a man alone in a crowd and his loneliness resulted in anger towards God, whom he blamed for putting him in that position. Even Moses' faith was overwhelmed by the physical and spiritual demands of leading that many people through a desert into a hostile land. And such people! *"Where am I to get* *enough food to feed these people?"* he asked God, echoing the very question the people were asking (11:4). And at last Moses threw up his hands and said, *"I am not able to bear all of these people alone. The burden is too heavy for me."* (11:15)

In such circumstances as these we observe that loneliness can have different manifestations. Not all lonely people are walking alone in the park or sitting up late at night watching movies or T.V. or crying themselves to sleep. Some are visibly and verbally angry.

Also we should be humbled and sobered that even those with Moses-caliber familiarity with God—extreme, miraculous, detailed knowledge—can be overwhelmed and crushed by the ordeal of living in a world like the one we live in.

In what sense was Moses alone? Certainly not in the sense that he was physically alone in that desert. He was among several million people, constantly! Also Moses had his brother and sister, Aaron and Miriam, with him. Moses words refer to the same type of loneliness that we saw in Genesis 2, where Adam did not find a suitable helper for himself among all of the creatures around him. Here, Moses lacked someone to carry the burden of leadership with him. The huge number of logistical, legal and civil responsibilities that fell on his shoulders every day were not being shared by anyone else, not even Aaron. And so he was crushed. When I wrote that last line I had a picture of a young mother with 4 young children, a household, 3 cats and 2 dogs and a busy husband to care for. And her aged mother needs her, too, as does the church and the little league. The right to life people, the leukemia fund drive and the Special Olympics folk all want her to assist them too. And then there's the upcoming high school reunion to plan. Every night she collapses into her bed, too tired to sleep and too conscious of what she didn't get done that day, and what awaits her at first light tomorrow. She and Moses are mad.

God's Response (Num. 11:16–17)

So what was God's response to Moses' angry, George Bailey-like prayer? He graciously offered Moses a remedy. As in

Genesis 2, this remedy for man's loneliness was a fellow man—
in fact, 70 fellow men (11:16).

Moses was to select 70 men from the elders of Israel, which
he knew to be mature and godly leaders. They were to already be
known for the characteristics they would need for the role God
was about to empower them to occupy.

Next, Moses was to bring them to the tabernacle of
meeting, in the center of camp, and stand there with them
(11:16). This would show the people that these men were
somehow or another to be identified with Moses. This was an
important part of making these fellow workers visually
acceptable to the fickle crowd.

At this point, God would take over (11:17). He would
empower the 70 with the same power He had given to Moses at
the start of his service. The source of this power was the Holy
Spirit. Then they would be able to bear the heavy burden with
Moses, resulting in Moses' prayer being resolved (11:14,15). God
told Moses that in doing all of this he would no longer bear the
burden of leadership alone (11:17).

Following this God addressed Moses' second concern,
regarding the food supply problem. We won't consider that at
present. But before leaving the passage altogether we should
note that *God's remedies did not immediately cure Moses*. Numbers
11:21–23 shows us just how deeply disturbed he was! With
God's kind and wise words still in his ears he challenged God's
ability to deliver on His promises, due to the extreme nature of
the needs they faced. God's response takes the form of a
question: *"Has the LORD's arm been shortened?"* This was a rebuke,
however velvetted and brief. God's reply has a most awesome
and challenging tone about it. Moses, too, would see just how
great God was, and if He could and would keep His word.

Let this remove from our minds any thought that the
Scriptures gives simplistic, unworkable solutions to unreal
people in a mythical world. No. The Bible world and the Bible
people were very real: as real as you and I. And God's remedies
seemed as impossible to them at first as they do to us here and
now. Nevertheless, He stands by His words and behind them, to
bring them to pass. Will we submit our minds and pride to Him?

I want to also reiterate that 11:21–23 shows us the extent to which Moses' faith had evaporated in his circumstances. The man who had brought Israel through the Red Sea, up from slavery in Egypt by his rod, here sounded more like the people he led than the God he served. He questioned God's ability, using statistics and common sense to jab at God.

Conclusions on Loneliness

Let's state some conclusions regarding loneliness from this sketch.

1. **Extreme pressure, in times of crisis, can reduce the strength of the most stable person into a state completely contrary to all of his previous behavior.**

2. **Prolonged exposure to people who drain you of strength can make you become like them.**

3. *Leadership* **is a burdensome position for anyone to be in alone.** This is true for those in parenting, business, church and/or government leadership.

4. **Loneliness can be** *seen by* **such traits as anger, death wishes, challenging God in basic faith areas, and self-absorbedness.**

5. **Once recognized, loneliness must be addressed as a matter for** *earnest prayer* **to God.** It isn't to be reasoned with or counseled about or ignored or buried under more work. We must take it to God, as boldly and nakedly as we can. This burden is for His ears first.

6. *God agrees* **with us when we see our limitations and He gives us others to supply our shortcomings.** Put differently, God does not always or often supply our need in times of loneliness with greater experiences of Himself *immediately* or without means—through dreams, visions,

voices and feelings—but *mediately*—through people and music and sights of created things.

7.   **God's solution for lonely leaders is not just to give them buddies, but to empower others with the Holy Spirit to take over responsibilities from them.** Leaders must be willing to give them their share of the load, which God has empowered them to do. They have to trust Him by trusting them, and give up the drive to control everything.

Summary

Moses' loneliness—a responsible person's loneliness—was the result of continual, extreme, and sometimes exotic demands placed upon him by his followers or dependents. Even if he or she is married and has family and friends to accompany him or her in life, the position may be so overwhelming that they become isolated, in their own minds. She may feel walled in. He may develop a martyr complex. "Woe is me" may be his frequent, unstated utterance. Or she may consider suicide as an alternative to living under such conditions. And the manifestation of this loneliness may be anger, directed at others, especially God.

Such a condition may be self-inflicted, if God has provided someone to share the load with and we don't let them, or if we don't ask Him to give us those empowered to work along side us.

INTERLUDE

THE SAINT MUST WALK ALONE

A. W. Tozer

The loneliness of the Christian results from his walk with God in an ungodly world, a walk that must often take him away from the fellowship of good Christians as well as from that of the unregenerate world. His God-given instincts cry out for companionship with others of his kind, others who can understand his longings, his aspirations, his absorption in the love of Christ. And because within his circle of friends there are so few who share his inner experiences he is forced to walk alone. The unsatisfied longings of the prophets for human understanding caused them to cry out in their complaint, and even our Lord Himself suffered in the same way.

The man [or woman] who has passed on into the divine Presence in actual inner experience will not find many who understand him. He finds few who care to talk about that which is the supreme object of his interest, so he is often silent and preoccupied in the midst of noisy religious shoptalk. For this he earns the reputation of being dull and over-serious, so he is avoided and the gulf between him and society widens. He searches for friends upon whose garments he can detect the smell of myrrh and aloes and cassia out of the ivory palaces, and finding few or none he, like Mary of old, keeps these things in his heart.

It is this very loneliness that throws him back upon God. His inability to find human companionship drives him to seek in God what he can find nowhere else.[12]

THE HAPPY EXCHANGE

Thomas Brooks

And as I desire that one of your eyes may be fixed upon her happiness—so I desire that your other eye may be fixed upon Christ's fullness. Though your brook be dried up, yet Christ the fountain of light, life, love, grace, glory, comfort, joy, goodness, sweetness and satisfaction—is still at hand—and always full and flowing—yes, overflowing!

As the worth and value of many pieces of silver is contracted in one piece of gold—so all the sweetness, all the goodness, all the excellencies which are in husbands, wives, children, friends, etc., are concentrated in Christ! Yes, all the whole volume of perfections which is spread through heaven and earth—is epitomized in Christ!

Oh, that your hearts and thoughts were thus busied about Christ, and taken up with Christ, and with those treasures of wisdom, knowledge, grace, goodness, sweetness, etc., which are in Him! This would very much allay your grief and sorrow, and keep your hearts quiet and silent before the Lord.[13]

---

[12] From an essay "The Saint Must Walk Alone" found in *Man—The Dwelling Place of God.*

[13] Quote from a sermon by Thomas Brooks, "A String of Pearls." This sermon was preached in London in 1657, at the funeral of that triumphant saint, Mrs. Mary Blake

CHAPTER 7

DISPLACED PERSONS

"Was ever grief like mine?"

—George Herbert

"If I had said, 'I will speak thus,' Behold, I would have been untrue to the generation of Your children. When I thought how to understand this, it was too painful for me."

—Psalm 73:15–16

This chapter has been a long time in coming! The last chapter was written approximately a year ago. A busy life has kept me from pursuing the topic of loneliness at all. Now that I can devote my mind to it a new category has grown up inside my mind and needing to find an outlet. This particular kind of loneliness has been a very prominent feature of my unguarded moments lately, so I come to it with some experience of the hollowness that is loneliness.

There is a type of loneliness that occurs to us due to unusual experiences we go through. They may be unusually traumatic (war, car wrecks, death of loved ones), unusually good (promotions, educational achievements, civic awards, wealth), or unusually spiritual (miracles, insight or service achievements). The experience moves us from one category or realm, where we have felt comfortable with our peers or family, into a realm where we cannot related to those same people or feel they cannot relate to us. Either way we have the sense of alienation or detachment or displacement. It is loneliness under whatever name. Many returning war veterans find they can only relate thoroughly to other veterans. Famous athletes or entertainers or businessmen may only feel relaxed around those who know their experiences firsthand. This partially explains the reason for interest oriented clubs and societies. There is a gravitation or magnetism toward those who share our interests and experiences and a converse repulsion or distancing from those who are unlike us, who can't understand from experience what our life is like.

If this all sounds snooty or uppity, it is. What I mean is that this is the soil from which bigotry, arrogance, and clannish exclusiveness grows. It is also the soil from which inferiority complexes and isolationism grows.

Examples from Scripture

Perhaps some specific examples from scripture can help us better grasp this form of loneliness.

Psalm 73

The passage quoted at the beginning of this chapter comes from the middle of a psalm written by Asaph, one of the ancient choir directors in the first temple period. In the psalm he bares his soul to the world and tells us the heart wrenching ordeal he went through. From what he tells us in 73:3–16 he was troubled by the unfairness of life, where the wicked prospered (3–12) while the godly missed out on the fun of this life by the rigorous pursuit of a non-existent life after death (13–14). What really made Asaph's pain worse was the sense of isolation he felt while among his fellow priests (15). He couldn't share his radical ideas with the other men who were dutifully carrying out their rituals in the temple, out of fear that he would offend them and poison them with his bitterness. He was alone with his experience, and that compounded his loneliness and pain. His thoughts were his alone and not even God could be told, or so he thought. And when we are speaking of loneliness or other emotional conditions, perception is as valid as fact. He got to the place where the pain was just too much for him. He was locked in a cell with himself as a cellmate, and he couldn't stand it much longer.

2 Corinthians 12:1–10

Paul's exceptional spiritual experiences were beyond words as far as the good they did him and others he ministered to. But they also brought him into the dangerous isolation zone: the place where few have gone and the few who do find themselves the exception to the rule. Unlike Asaph, Paul was not in danger of cursing God and dying but of being lifted up with pride or conceit from his unusual privilege. And this would have resulted in much harm to others and dishonor to the God who gave him the gifts. And that would have led to sore chastisement after the fact.

Psalm 42:1–11

The unknown writer of this psalm cites his unusually joyous access to God's worship place as a contributing cause to his present distress. He was once able to be near God's worship and worshippers. But now he was living the life of an exile among scornful unbelievers (1–3). His isolation was not just geographic but experiential. He had tasted high privilege and could no longer be happy with lesser things, even though everyone else around him was well adjusted.

Ecclesiastes 1:16–18

Solomon does not explain exactly what it is about learning that increases the learner's sorrow. As the book unfolds, however, it becomes clear that at least one thing he did mean in 1:18 was that being more aware of the true picture of *"life under the sun"* brought more vexation to him who had gained the insight. As a speculation may it not also have been in Solomon's mind that not many were as aware or enlightened as he was, making him one of the few people who could observe *"life under the sun"* and so bringing him double vexation. Not only was he aware that life is full of a strange mixture of good and bad, in its season, and that no amount of pleasure or achievement could alter the sure and relentless approach of death but he was one of the few who really knew this about life and saw through the spin everyone else puts on life. He knew and he knew that he knew in isolation from his fellow men. His wealth, position and spiritual gift made him very unique among mankind of all times. Unique people can get very lonely.

Psalm 142:4

Another place where this type of loneliness is voiced is near the end of the book of Psalms. The descriptive superscription attributes this psalm to David and was written during one of his many episodes of fleeing from someone and hiding in cave. Of all the places that evoke smells and sounds and sensations to anyone with an imagination, caves probably are right at the top of the list. Why did David have to flee? Wasn't it due to God's choosing him to be king over Israel during the reign of Saul? God's "gift" of promotion to a high position resulted in David having to run for his life when the current king refused to accept God's will and attempting to derail it by killing the boy-usurper, his harpist, David. From the sounds of 142:4 David is very, very alone. He knows of no other human being who cares for his soul or life.

~~ℰ∂~~

The list of passages could go on. But it is evident to me that it is a valid experience of people throughout history to struggle inwardly with a sense of displacement or dislocation when they experience traumatic or unique things along the pathway.

Examples from My Life

About 8 years ago I was given a library that had belonged to a friend's dad. When I went to pick it up there, to my amazement, was an extensive collection of Puritan authors. Long before I had wished for such books, but I could never afford them, and the ability to wish in me had gradually ceased along with the appetite for books. But now, thrust into my life, was this valuable library. I was both joyful and bewildered. Why had God given me this <u>now</u> and what was I (a painter) to do with it?

I began reading some of them: Jeremiah Burroughs, John Owen, Richard Baxter, Thomas Watson, Dr. Gill, Pink, Henry. I got on the internet and found websites dedicated to Puritan and reformed writings and I downloaded thousands of pages of sermons and books and then read those. Not since my seminary days had I read so much thought-provoking material. And even then the reading had not caused the holy upheaval the Puritans generated in my life.

As I write this chapter I do so fully and painfully aware that few other people in my circle have read or will read the wealth of Puritan thinking. The majority of people I preach to week in and week out have no idea such things exist and others hope they never have any idea what the great saints of the past have believed. Here I am, burning on the inside like a furnace fed by jet fuel and walking among those who thrive on the shallows, falling in step behind whatever pied piper appears in the Christian bookstore or on the religious station.

My sensation is one of loneliness. Not a self righteous or arrogant know-it-allness but a sadness, a "what's the use" chill that is increasingly tempting me to isolate myself from my surroundings. Do you know what I mean?

A second anecdote from life may further deepen the reader's grasp of the phenomenon of this type of loneliness. Last year I went to a wedding and sat next to a brother I hadn't seen in some time. In the course of catching up he told me he had discovered the writings of Martin Luther and was just overwhelmed with them. He was presently immersed in a personal mission to make one of Luther's favorite topics readable for today's audience.

As I listened to him ooh and aah about the various aspects of it all and what it had done to him already I noticed a growing desire in me to warn him of where this would take him. So when he was done and waiting for me to pick up the conversation I said, "I'm really excited for you. I look forward to reading your work when you are done. Keep at it and don't give up. But be warned. The road you are traveling on here is a very lonely one. You will not find very many who will share your joy or think the time and energy well spent on a guy 500 years dead. Prepare for a lonely journey."

He asked for an explanation, but the wedding was starting by then so I had to postpone the longer version of what this chapter is addressing. Unique experiences lead to a kind of loneliness or solitude.

Solace for Displaced People

What about some solace? Is there no balm to help us? Are we sentenced to wander the earth as though we were perfect strangers to the rest of the pilgrims of life?

Psalm 142

Take Psalm 142 for some insight into the helps God has provided for displaced persons. David tells that though no man cared for his soul, as far as he knew, God was the exception for exceptional people (142:1, 2, 3, 5, 6). He excludes God from the list of those who had abandoned him and looks to Him as the only one who could and would provide refuge and help to him. David discovered or rediscovered that the LORD knew his path, the way he walked and what he was going through (3) and so he was not completely alone.

But what good does that do? Can a mortal find comfort and companionship from the invisible omnipresence and omniscience of the immortal Creator? Verse 7 indicates that the answer is a categorical "yes"! Such awareness generates hope in David as he crouches in the cave with the scorpions and rats and bats. He pins his future hopes of fellowship with his companions on God's sheltering him in the present, invisible though He may be.

And how does David draw on God for strength and help against his loneliness and his real attackers? By talking to Him (1, 2, 5, 6). When there is no one else to converse with and share your heartaches and fears what do you do? Do you talk to

95

yourself? Do you write out your thoughts in your diary? Do you blog to a world of strangers? David found that total displacement from other mortals actually gave him one on One, undistracted access with God and the drive to take advantage of the access. Hmm. I wonder if God designed it that way?

Psalms 42 and 43

What about Psalm 42 and 43? How did that dislocated has-been find solace to keep his head above the rising tide of despair? Psalm 42:5–11 shows us his approach to his dilemma.

First, he challenged himself, he debated himself as to the reason for his melancholy outlook. He demands reasons for such feelings. "Why are you like this, my soul," he says. When no one else is able to enter into my world of thought, when I feel like I am somewhere no one else has been before and that no one else can relate with me in my experience I still have one person I can talk to and engage in dialogue—myself. In this case the conversation was confrontational. The writer's reasonable side would not allow his feeling side to continue to steer a course towards the reef of despair unchallenged. "Hey there! What do you think you're doing, moping around like this?"

Second, he does what David did in Psalm 142 (42:6, 7, 9, 10). He tells God all about his troubles and appeals to Him for help.

Psalm 73

In Psalm 73, Asaph's turning point is described in the verse following his plaintive cry *"When I thought how to understand this it was too painful for me"*. When he went into the sanctuary where he served as a temple choir director and musician he saw something that changed his whole demeanor and brought him to a resolution totally different from where he was headed. Instead of letting his isolation lead to disabling depression he just went to work anyway and it was while there, doing the stuff that had just seemed so pointless and vain (73:13) that the light dawned on him. Indeed, the prosperous wicked were traveling footloose and fancy free, skating along with no moral or theological handicaps to inhibit their business gains. He could admit that that observation was both accurate and part of God's design. That's **step one**.

Secondly, he was able to see past today and remember that there is a future everyone must face, and with it, the God of judgment. That's when the footloose and fancy free slip off of the edge of the precipice into a chasm of destruction (18). No amount of momentary prosperity can begin to compensate the soul that is lost forever.

Thirdly, Asaph spoke to God about these things (21–28). As in the previous two accounts the dislocated, lonely soul converses with God at some point in the experience. In this case it is a grand confession of how blessed he really was all along, although he hadn't realized it before. One of the things he cites to corroborate his new assessment is that he was *"continually with You. You hold me by my right hand. You will guide me with Your counsel and afterward receive me to glory."* *(23, 24)* Notice these strong statements of companionship Asaph had and contrast them with his previous feelings of isolation (15, 16).

You may wonder, as I did, what it was that Asaph saw in the sanctuary that caused his turn around. Opinion has differed about that over the centuries, as commentaries show. Some think Asaph actually had a transporting experience like Paul did in 2 Corinthians 12 which brought him into the very sanctuary where God is enthroned. Others think Asaph was referring to illumination by the Holy Spirit of the word of God, the sanctuary where God's presence is conveyed most clearly to the observant soul. There in divine doctrine, these interpreters think, Asaph saw what before he had not seen.

Personally, I think the sanctuary spoken of was the same one Asaph worked in as choir director. He saw something or heard something in that building dedicated to God's worship that redirected him and salvaged a wrecked mind and recycled it into a stronger model, well-suited for the harsh realities of a real world. What it was is not clear and we can only speculate.

But we are not left in doubt about what thought was suddenly awakened in his mind by the view. He remembered that there is a future, and the future for wicked makes any pleasure or success or gain in this life a weight that makes their

97

forever even more burdensome than if they had not prospered. Conversely, the future of the righteous is bright and secure, making any suffering endured on the way, in this life, bearable and even reasonable (73:18–28).

2 Corinthians 12

With regards to 2 Corinthians 12 and Paul's famous, mysterious *"thorn in the flesh"* notice again that his ordeal was resolved when he persistently prayed about it. True, the resolution was not one that supports the prosperity gospel premise that God always wants us healthy and wealthy. But Christ's verbal answer enabled Paul to live with his disability, bringing more glory to Christ thereby (9,10). Paul valued the supply of Christ's virtue over all other things, even health, and his life continued to be one fruitfully useful to the Holy Spirit, despite his toxic levels of special revelation.

Hebrews 2:14–18 and 4:14–16

One last passage should be considered before finishing this treatment of displaced persons. Hebrews 2:14–18 and 4:14–16 informs us that one of the designs God the Father had in the incarnation of God the Son was to equip Him for His role as High Priest between Himself and His people. In the words of C. S. Lewis' demon, Screwtape, when speaking about the inability of spirit-beings to understand humans *"Oh that abominable advantage of the Enemy* (God)." He was talking about the incarnation. Now that God has experienced creaturehood, His omniscience supplemented by incarnation and real life ordeals, He is the only Person both able and willing to enter into all of our situations. Thereby Jesus Christ has become the One person we can never be isolated from by exotic experiences. The indwelling Holy Spirit assists us when words fail us (Rom. 8:26, 27) so that even if we are cut off from family, our fellow man or even from our own bodily functions (e.g. vegetable states, paralysis, Alzheimer's disease) we can have the consciousness of One who understands and cares and is with us right where we are, through it all (Ps. 23:2–4).

So **one thing** we should be doing regularly is stockpiling our minds with detailed awareness of the life of Jesus Christ while He was on earth. The more we know and meditate on His experience among us the better able we will be to find in Him an understanding and strong priest. To assist the reader in this I have included a classic *poem by George Herbert at the end of this chapter. As Herbert contemplated the Lord Jesus' experience he ended each quatrain with the same tag line: "Was ever grief like mine?" The expected answer to this rhetorical question from the Savior is obvious.

But did He experience sin? Did He experience childbirth? Did He experience every single thing every human being has experienced? No (Heb. 4:15). But neither has any human being experience everything every other human being has experienced. But we have had the human experience. That's what makes us human.

And as for His not experiencing sin firsthand I would like to remind the objector that Christ experienced sin by living amongst sinners. By obeying God He knew firsthand what the tree of the knowledge of good and evil was about. Had Adam chosen that alternative he would have truly gained the knowledge he sought to gain through disobedience. On the cross, Christ experienced the guilt of sin and weight of wrath for sin like no other human has or can. So in reality, though Christ didn't personally sin and could not do so, He is nonetheless more experienced with sin than any human being. So He is better able to draw near to us in the times when we sin and help us with the guilt and weight we are carrying.

Another thing to do is to remember that we shouldn't put more weight on our fellow man than they were made to carry. Trucks and trains aren't the only things with capacity limits. I shouldn't blame people for not having experienced my personal sensations and appetites. If I would consistently apply this understanding to other people I would realize they are probably feeling the same way about me! They probably are wondering why I'm not more in tune with them and their issues and concerns. And so here we are, sitting across the table from one another; isolated within hugging distance of each other; imagining that we are each so different from everyone else that we might as well live with the wild animals rather than with our own kind.

And think of this: who has had more unique experiences than God? Or who is essentially more different than God? One of the components of the idea of holiness is that of set-apartness or uniqueness. There is no other God but Him and no one can begin to fathom what it is like to be God. Only as He gives us experiences and instructions can we gain insight into Him. For example, the prophet Hosea was told to marry an unfaithful woman to show Israel what God was going through with them, His unfaithful bride (Hos. 1–3).

So is God completely isolated and lonely? Was it because He was lonely that He created angels and mankind? On the contrary, it was because He was in perfect fellowship with Himself, as a triune being, that He was never lonely or isolated. He created out of His fullness, like a spring tends to overflow its shoreline and water the surrounding countryside. It is no flaw in God to want beings capable of enjoying Him in worshipping Him. And His greatest joy is in the knowledge of Himself, the greatest good and only God. When we are most cut off from all others, or at least when we think we are cut off from all others, we have yet to reach the limits of God's ability to know us, through and through. We are at that moment in a position to enter, alone, into the Holy of holies, into the darkness where the mercy seat rests, overshadowed by the outstretched wings of the cherubim. We are to come boldly now, and come as often as necessity compels us, and enter there where sits One on the mercy seat who can be touched by the feeling of our infirmities because He was touched in those same areas Himself. May every event in our lives fuse us to Him and not drive us from Him.

INTERLUDE

THE SACRIFICE

George Herbert

Oh all ye, who pass by, whose eyes and mind
To worldly things are sharp, but to me blind;
To me, who took eyes that I might you find:
    Was ever grief like mine?

The Princes of my people make a head
Against their Maker: they do wish me dead,
Who cannot wish, except I give them bread:
    Was ever grief like mine?

Without me each one, who doth now me brave,
Had to this day been an Egyptian slave.
They use that power against me, which I gave:
    Was ever grief like mine?

Mine own Apostle, who the bag did bear,
Though he had all I had, did not forebear
To sell me also, and to put me there:
    Was ever grief like mine?

For thirty pence he did my death devise,
Who at three hundred did the ointment prize,
Not half so sweet as my sweet sacrifice:
 Was ever grief like mine?

Therefore my soul melts, and my heart's dear treasure
Drops blood (the only beads) my words to measure:
O let this cup pass, if it be thy pleasure:
 Was ever grief like mine?

These drops being temper'd with a sinner's tears,
A Balsam are for both the Hemispheres:
Curing all wounds but mine; all, but my fears,
 Was ever grief like mine?

Yet my Disciples sleep: I cannot gain
One hour of watching; but their drowsy brain
Comforts not me, and doth my doctrine stain:
 Was ever grief like mine?

Arise, arise, they come. Look how they run.
Alas! what haste they make to be undone!
How with their lanterns do they seek the sun!
 Was ever grief like mine?

With clubs and staves they seek me, as a thief,
Who am the way of truth, the true relief;
Most true to those, who are my greatest grief:
 Was ever grief like mine?

Judas, dost thou betray me with a kiss?
Canst thou find hell about my lips? and miss
Of life, just at the gates of life and bliss?
 Was ever grief like mine?

See, they lay hold on me, not with the hands
Of faith, but fury: yet at their commands

I suffer binding, who have loos'd their bands:
  Was ever grief like mine?

All my Disciples fly; fear puts a bar
Betwixt my friends and me. They leave the star
That brought the wise men of the East from far.
  Was ever grief like mine?

Then from one ruler to another bound
They lead me; urging, that it was not sound
What I taught: Comments would the text confound.
  Was ever grief like mine?

The Priest and rulers all false witness seek
'Gainst him, who seeks not life, but is the meek
And ready Paschal Lamb of this great week:
  Was ever grief like mine?

Then they accuse me of great blasphemy,
  That I did thrust into the Deity,
Who never thought that any robbery:
  Was ever grief like mine?

Some said, that I the Temple to the floor
In three days raz'd, and raised as before.
Why, he that built the world can do much more:
  Was ever grief like mine?

Then they condemn me all with that same breath,
  Which I do give them daily, unto death.
  Thus Adam my first breathing rendereth:
  Was ever grief like mine?

They bind, and lead me unto Herod: he
Sends me to Pilate. This makes them agree;
But yet their friendship is my enmity:
  Was ever grief like mine?

Herod and all his bands do set me light,
Who teach all hands to war, fingers to fight,
And only am the Lord of hosts and might:
  Was ever grief like mine?

Herod in judgment sits while I do stand;
Examines me with a censorious hand:
I him obey, who all things else command:
  Was ever grief like mine?

The Jews accuse me with despitefulness;
And vying malice with my gentleness,
Pick quarrels with their only happiness:
  Was ever grief like mine?

I answer nothing, but with patience prove
If stony hearts will melt with gentle love.
But who does hawk at eagles with a dove?
  Was ever grief like mine?

My silence rather doth augment their cry;
My dove doth back into my bosom fly;
Because the raging waters still are high:
  Was ever grief like mine?

Hark how they cry aloud still, 'Crucify:
It is not fit he live a day, ' they cry,
Who cannot live less than eternally:
  Was ever grief like mine?

Pilate a stranger holdeth off; but they,
Mine own dear people, cry, 'Away, away, '
With noises confused frighting the day:
  Was ever grief like mine?

Yet still they shout, and cry, and stop their ears,
Putting my life among their sins and fears,

And therefore wish my blood on them and theirs:
   Was ever grief like mine?

See how spite cankers things. These words aright
Used, and wished, are the whole world's light:
But honey is their gall, brightness their night:
   Was ever grief like mine?

They choose a murderer, and all agree
In him to do themselves a courtesy:
For it was their own cause who killed me:
   Was ever grief like mine?

And a seditious murderer he was:
But I the Prince of peace; peace that doth pass
All understanding, more than heav'n doth glass:
   Was ever grief like mine?

Why, Caesar is their only King, not I:
He clave the stony rock, when they were dry;
But surely not their hearts, as I well try:
   Was ever grief like mine?

Ah! how they scourge me! yet my tenderness
Doubles each lash: and yet their bitterness
Winds up my grief to a mysteriousness.
   Was ever grief like mine?

They buffet me, and box me as they list,
Who grasp the earth and heaven with my fist,
And never yet, whom I would punish, miss'd:
   Was ever grief like mine?

Behold, they spit on me in scornful wise,
Who by my spittle gave the blind man eyes,
Leaving his blindness to mine enemies:
   Was ever grief like mine?

My face they cover, though it be divine.
As Moses' face was veiled, so is mine,
Lest on their double-dark souls either shine:
    Was ever grief like mine?

Servants and abjects flout me; they are witty:
'Now prophesy who strikes thee, ' is their ditty.
So they in me deny themselves all pity:
    Was ever grief like mine?

And now I am deliver'd unto death,
Which each one calls for so with utmost breath,
That he before me well nigh suffereth:
    Was ever grief like mine?

Weep not, dear friends, since I for both have wept
When all my tears were blood, the while you slept:
Your tears for your own fortunes should be kept:
    Was ever grief like mine?

The soldiers lead me to the common hall;
There they deride me, they abuse me all:
Yet for twelve heavenly legions I could call:
    Was ever grief like mine?

Then with a scarlet robe they me array;
Which shows my blood to be the only way.
And cordial left to repair man's decay:
    Was ever grief like mine?

Then on my head a crown of thorns I wear:
For these are all the grapes Sion doth bear,
Though I my vine planted and watred there:
    Was ever grief like mine?

So sits the earth's great curse in Adam's fall
Upon my head: so I remove it all

From th' earth unto my brows, and bear the thrall:
    Was ever grief like mine?

Then with the reed they gave to me before,
They strike my head, the rock from whence all store
  Of heavn'ly blessings issue evermore:
    Was ever grief like mine?

They bow their knees to me, and cry, 'Hail king':
  What ever scoffs or scornfulness can bring,
  I am the floor, the sink, where they it fling:
    Was ever grief like mine?

Yet since man's sceptres are as frail as reeds,
And thorny all their crowns, bloody their weeds;
  I, who am Truth, turn into truth their deeds:
    Was ever grief like mine?

The soldiers also spit upon that face,
  Which Angels did desire to have the grace,
And Prophets once to see, but found no place:
    Was ever grief like mine?

Thus trimmed forth they bring me to the rout,
Who 'Crucify him, ' cry with one strong shout.
God holds his peace at man, and man cries out.
    Was ever grief like mine?

They lead me in once more, and putting then
Mine own clothes on, they lead me out again.
Whom devils fly, thus is he toss'd of men:
    Was ever grief like mine?

And now weary of sport, glad to engross
All spite in one, counting my life their loss,
  They carry me to my most bitter cross
    Was ever grief like mine?

My cross I bear my self, until I faint:
Then Simon bears it for me by constraint,
The decreed burden of each mortal Saint:
    Was ever grief like mine?

O all ye who pass by, behold and see;
Man stole the fruit, but I must climb the tree;
The tree of life to all, but only me:
    Was ever grief like mine?

Lo, here I hang, charg'd with a world of sin,
The greater world o' th' two; for that came in
By words, but this by sorrow I must win:
    Was ever grief like mine?

Such sorrow, as if sinful man could feel,
Or feel his part, he would not cease to kneel,
Till all were melted, though he were all steel;
    Was ever grief like mine?

But, O my God, my God! why leav'st thou me,
The son, in whom thou dost delight to be?
    My God, my God—
    Never was grief like mine.

Shame tears my soul, my body many a wound;
Sharp nails pierce this, but sharper that confound;
Reproaches, which are free, while I am bound.
    Was ever grief like mine?

Now heal thy self, Physician; now come down.
Alas! I did so, when I left my crown
And father's smile for you, to feel his frown:
    Was ever grief like mine?

In healing not my self, there doth consist
All that salvation, which ye now resist;

Your safety in my sickness doth subsist:
    Was ever grief like mine?

Betwixt two thieves I spend my utmost breath,
  As he that for some robbery suffereth.
  Alas! what have I stolen from you? death:
    Was ever grief like mine?

A king my title is, prefixt on high;
  Yet by my subjects am condemn'd to die
  A servile death in servile company;
    Was ever grief like mine?

They gave me vinegar mingled with gall,
  But more with malice: yet, when they did call,
  With Manna, Angels' food, I fed them all:
    Was ever grief like mine?

They part my garments, and by lot dispose
  My coat, the type of love, which once cur'd those
  Who sought for help, never malicious foes:
    Was ever grief like mine?

Nay, after death their spite shall further go;
  For they will pierce my side, I full well know;
  That as sin came, so Sacraments might flow:
    Was ever grief like mine?

But now I die; now all is finished.
  My woe, man's weal: and now I bow my head.
  Only let others say, when I am dead,
    Never was grief like mine.

CHAPTER 8

OF ANGELS AND DEMONS

Is Satan lonely? Do the fallen angels (the demons) experience loneliness? For that matter do the unfallen angels experience loneliness or its opposite, the fullness of fellowship?

For some time now I've been preparing to include a chapter on the devil and loneliness, intending it to be a treatment of his work in producing or magnifying loneliness in humans. But a different idea has furrowed my brow and sent me back to my Bible for answers. What about Satan as a sufferer of loneliness?

Shouldn't we begin at the beginning? Since the angel called Satan or the devil was, like man, created by God and, like man, was originally good, his rebellion and fall from the heights rendered him both a casualty and a causality of sin. Romans 5:20 refers to *sin*, not Satan, as the opponent of God's grace, saying *"But where sin abounded, grace abounded much more."* In the whole context of Romans 5–7 it is evil that God has triumphed over in Christ. Satan and the fallen angels and fallen man and all the bi-products of sin fall under the headline **"God's grace defeats sin"**.

While Satan is called the god of this world (2 Cor. 4:3, 4) and the one for whom hell was designed, he himself is the committer of the original sin, the first to fall and lie shattered by his sin. His fall, like Adam's, forced expulsion from God's favor.

Was he that was made to draw nourishment and fullness from God, like man, reduced by his sedition to emptiness and self-concealment and finding companionship among his co-conspirators, also like man? Was he the first to experience the vanity of vanities, the emptiness of empty living under the sun, trying to find make up from the shards of creation for fullness of God, now lost? (Isa. 14:9–15; Ezek. 28:13–19)

Adam and Eve did not wander from God by the influence of anything He had done or made but from the seduction of that seduced angel. They distorted the image of God by following the prince of distortion, himself having partaken first of forbidden fruit and its consequences. They became like their adopted father (John 8:44). Their estrangement from God, their alienation from harmony, their finding frustration in the world once made to be their garden mirrored Satan's own estrangement, alienation, and frustration. All who are victims of sin are partakers of sin's consequences, and that includes sin's first casualty, Satan.

This chapter is not an attempt to generate sympathy for the devil or to deny he is sin's greatest promoter. Rather it is an attempt to explain how it came to be that God's good creation crashed and what the repercussions are on all of creation. If Satan was always Satan (the accuser) then God would be the author of evil. But God created angels and humans good, and each rank experienced dissension and civil war. One rank, fallen angels, sought dominion and/or alliance with the next rank below them, humans. Both have been reeling in the aftermath of the dislocation ever since. Angels and men experience loneliness, estrangement, emptiness, vanity.

Consider the Biblical evidence for the preceding claims:

1. The angels all shouted for joy at creation (Job 38:7).

2. Fallen angels seek to live in a host. They left their "first habitation" to live with human females in sexual pleasures that produced offspring (Jude 6; Gen. 6:1–6).

3. The angels regularly appear before God to give account of their actions (Job 1:6ff and 2:1ff) and in both of these instances those actions had to do with the world of men.

4. The fallen angels tend to gravitate to possessing human bodies as a host. Consider Mark 5:1–20, Luke 11:15–28 and all of the other NT possession accounts. The

demons begged not to be cast out of a human host into the abyss and they would prefer to live in the bodies of swine than to go to the abyss or be bodiless.

5. Unlike unfallen man (Adam), angels were not created in need of mates nor were they given marriage as an institution for companionship (Matt. 22: 30; Luke 20:36). The celibacy of angels serves as a template for the future of all glorified humans. They have no built in need for helpmates yet to be created from their ribs, if they have ribs. Apparently, their number was complete at God's creative act and no new angels have been created or reproduced since that time.

6. Contrary to our tendency to demonize demons, they do not always drive people to madness or anti-social behavior. In Acts 16:16–19 the demonized girl was in a business relationship with some men who used her supernatural powers to make money. In Mark 1:21–28 we find a demonized man attending the synagogue where Jesus was. The man wanted Jesus to leave them alone (plural), probably meaning the people in attendance, but in view of other passages he may also have meant the other demons present. Judas Iscariot was invaded by Satan himself (John 13:27) and that union led Judas to go to his co-conspirators to get a detachment of soldiers to arrest Jesus. My point here is not that these are good actions but that these people were not frothing and raging and wild, as we often imagine all demonizations to be.

7. However, in at least one particularly well-known case demons did cause some men to act wildly and dangerously. Matthew 8:28–34, Mark 5:1–20 and Luke 8:26–40 give parallel accounts of the Gadarene demoniac or demoniacs, as Matthew tells. Apparently one was the spokesman and more prominent of the two, so Mark and Luke focus only on him. But in fact

there were two of them. Notice the description of their behavior:

- They lived among the dead. Luke 8:29 tells us the demon was responsible for this solitary and sad abode.
- They were fierce or violent to anyone who came near them or attempted to restrain them.
- They were naked.
- They were uncontrollable, having superhuman strength to break any device used to bind them.
- This was a chronic problem, that is, it didn't happen now and then. They were always like this. Night and day they lived there and behaved like this.
- They cut themselves with stones in torment (see Mark 9:14–27).
- They cried out with loud voices.
- They confronted Jesus, recognized His divine person and begged Him to not send the demon horde from the human hosts into the abyss (Luke 4:33, 41).

It is intriguing to read these accounts and notice how, at Jesus' command to leave, the singular demon is suddenly spoken of in the plural (see chart on next page).

Taken all in all, as I do in such instances, the whole picture seems to be that two men, with multiple demons are involved. One of them was more prominent or the spokesman of the two. Their general condition was that of being demonized, and in fact they were demonized by a vast horde of demons.

Their <u>condition</u> was singular—demonized—but the <u>actual number</u> of demons responsible for their condition was legion (see Luke 11:24–26). Thus, due to the influence of these unclean spirits, the men were driven away from the society of their families and friends to dwell among the only humans that were safe from their tirades, the dead. Their behavior was the cause of their isolation.

Singular	Plural
Luke 8:29 "the unclean spirit" "the demon"	**Luke 8:30, 31** "many demons had entered him" "they begged Him"
Mark 5:2 "an unclean spirit"	**Mark 5:10** "he begged Him earnestly that He would not send them out of the country" **Mark 5:12,13** "So all the demons begged Him, 'Send us to the swine that we may enter them.' So Jesus gave them permission."
*Matthew's account has both **plural men** and **plural demons,** but is vague as to whether there were multiple demons in each demoniac or one demon per man.*	

Before leaving this item it is important to contrast the activities of the holy angels with the scene we just considered. Throughout God's Word the unfallen, holy angels appear as the consolers and helpers of men. When Elijah fled from Jezebel into the wilderness he was twice fed by an angel and encouraged on his journey to meet with God (1 Kings 19:1–8). The angel Gabriel was especially helpful to Daniel (Dan. 8:16–19, 9:20–23, 10:5–21) in the realm of giving understanding to the prophet in the extreme visions he had of the future. The activities of angels in the Gospels are well known, especially at the resurrection, and let us not forget that was an angel that appeared to Christ in Gethsemane and encouraged Him. Lastly, the Revelation has more mention of angels than any one book in the Bible, and while their activities are not exclusively peaceful, they are always in submission to the triune God, and therefore good for the godly.

114

To sum up for a moment so as to avoid confusion, let me conclude that #6 and #7 give us a total picture of the way demonization is manifested. It can be either the stereotypical kind, like the Gadarenes or king Saul or the more sociably acceptable kind, like Judas Iscariot or the pagan festivals of public immorality or drunkenness.

Now, to continue considering the biblical evidence:

8. Spiritual beings, like angels or demons, are not limited or "crowded" by physical constraints. Though they can live without bodies they prefer to be hosted in a physical body. This is true of the fallen angels, since they are the ones who revolted and left their submissive roles, as God had designed (see Luke 11:24–26) The holy angels are not spoken of as possessing other forms than their own, which, in some cases has a human appearance (Acts 1:10). But some of them have very unique forms (See Isaiah 6:2; Ezekiel 1:5–14; Revelation 4:6–8).

9. Satan's kingdom, as all kingdoms, can only endure where there is unity among its parts or members (Luke 11: 22–24). Thus the fallen angels fell from fellowship with God into a fellowship or communion or kingdom of evil, organized to preserve itself in unity (see Ephesians 1:21, 2:10, 6:12). C. S. Lewis called it the "Lowerarchy"!

10. The methods fallen angels use, in their well-organized team effort to oppose God and replace Him, may vary—but the goal does not. If a person can be alienated or kept alienated from God and his fellow man by being driven into sinful isolation—living in the tombs, unrestrained and bleeding from self-inflicted wounds—then that device accomplishes the goal. If a person can be made drunk with success, riches and fame and be overcome with the cares of this life to the complete disregard for the eternity to come, then that

method also realizes the single goal of robbing God of His glory. Guilt can also serve their purpose.

Consider the case of the man in 1 Corinthians 5:1–5 and 2 Corinthians 2:3–11 we have another insight into the devil and his influence on human isolation, which leads to loneliness. I take the view that the man under discussion for restoration to the church in 2 Corinthians 2 was the same man who was earlier excommunicated by the church at Paul's urging in 1 Corinthians 5. Not everyone agrees with this hypothesis, but still I think there are good reasons to connect the two. If this is the case then after Paul's first letter was acted on in Corinth and the man was removed from the fellowship of the believers he became convicted of his sins and repented and was seeking reinstatement to the warm and uplifting fellowship of the church. But the problem was that they weren't as ready to extend forgiveness and restoration as he was to ask for it. So Paul, by the Holy Spirit's inspiration has to write and urge them to receive him back. In doing so he warns them against banishing a repentant brother, for fear of what Satan might do with the circumstances, climaxing his appeal with these words, "lest Satan should take advantage of us; for we are not ignorant of his devices" (2 Cor. 2:11).

What devices does Paul mean? How would Satan take advantage of this situation? Paul had already told them in 2:7, "so that, on the contrary, you ought rather to forgive and comfort him, lest perhaps such a one be swallowed up with too much sorrow." It seems to me Paul was warning the church against making the mistake of treating this man like the demoniacs of Gadara, who were driven by demons to live in banishment from society. Satan's tactics in this case would be to drown the repentant man in guilt and despair, when the fellowship of Christians was withheld from him. Satan would use his isolation to take advantage and overwhelm him, perhaps even to his self-destruction. This would be death by loneliness.

Conclusion

We may be shocked to read in Mark 1:12 that the Holy Spirit, who had just descended from heaven as a dove and lighted upon the Lord Jesus Christ immediately drove or sent Christ into the wilderness for the expressed purpose of exposing Him to Satan's temptation. Have you taken that all in? The Gadarenes, the man in 2 Corinthians and the Lord Jesus all driven into banishment, into barren places, exposed to the devil's agenda. The same One who is stampeded by the Spirit into the wilderness to meet Satan head on, later rescued men whom Satan's hordes had driven into the wilderness, which led to a pig stampede and death for them but new life for the men. He who *was ministered to by angels* after His temptation in the wilderness (Mark 1:13) *ministered to* the demonized his own clothes and good counsel. Luke 22:43 informs us that an angel came to assist or strengthen the solitary Christ in Gethsemane, while His three best disciples slept. He was not alone, and He promised never to leave or forsake His own, to be tormented by Satan undefended.

Hebrews 12:22–24 lists the glorious nature of the city of God, the heavenly Jerusalem, in which the humble believers have citizenship. No longer strangers (Eph. 2:19–22) we shall then fully experience the never before experienced wonder of fellowship with the holy angels and the equally blessed removal of fellowship with the fallen angels (Rev. 20:1–3, 7–15, 21:27, 22:15). That fellowship will be in fullness of all joy and in the right relationship of Creator to creature, all creatures to all other creatures, without time constraints and minus all of sin's fruits.

The fellowship the fallen angels and fallen, unredeemed men have is an unspeakable horror. Every time it comes up in sacred writings it evokes the most extreme language imaginable: *weeping, wailing, gnashing of teeth, where the worm does not die and the fire is never quenched, place of torments, unslaked thirst, outer darkness, everlasting destruction.* The unholy angels are both the instruments that aggravate human misery and loneliness, even to the point of everlasting banishment and also the sufferers of loneliness themselves. The holy angels are also both instruments and

117

participants in human fulfillment. They are appointed as the guardians of saved sinners (Heb. 1:14; Matt. 18:10) and only in their company will our full blessedness be experienced.

Therefore, believers in Christ are admonished to be considerate of strangers, who have left the familiar and safe to make Christ known. We are to be mindful of those prisoners who are suffering the loss of their liberty and other tortures for Christ's sake (Heb. 13:1–3). Why? In the case of welcoming strangers it is because some in the past, in welcoming the wandering into their homes have found themselves caring for angels (see Gen. 18:2–15 and Judges 13:2–7). And as for those who are imprisoned and cut off from the society of their friends and family, who are most susceptible to despair from loneliness, we are reminded that they, too, are still part of the body that we belong to. When one part suffers the whole body suffers. A dislocated pinky toe is commiserated and cared for by all of the body's functions. So, too, must travelers and prisoners for Christ's sake be cared for.

INTERLUDE

THE PIT

Elizabeth

The enshrouding blackness engulfs me.
Alone
Afraid
My mind a whirlpool
Ever inwards
Towards an eternity of intolerable pain

I used to reach out a hand
Into the black unknown
In hope
But my soul was torn from me
And I hoped no more

It was like a pit
Unfathomable depth
Torturous groveling
My tears the only sound
In the impenetrable darkness

I remember that pit
And the fear
And the hopelessness
Of an eternal agony of mind

INTERLUDE

And the soulless wandering
In an uncharted desert

Now

I find myself at this oasis
This unlooked-for harbor
This refuge
I did not deserve that gracious act
To pluck me
From that all-powerful deep

I had no hope
But turning back along the path I came
I see a gracious hand
And a loving smile
I see a guiding light
And feel a protecting

Nestling in your warmth
My cold heart has thawed
The blackness of my soul
Has blossomed into a million blooms
My tears have turned to jewels
And my bitterness to honey
But I remember the pit
Keep me, O Lord
Safe
In the refuge of your wings

CHAPTER 9

PHANTOM CRUTCHES

I was riding home with my Dad the other day from my Mom's knee surgery. Conversation between us was taking a nap in the back seat, so as the Ohio countryside sped past us he put in a CD of country favorites and we spent the time swerving down memory lane. Now these were *classic* country hits, so there were lots of heart-broken jilted lovers, defiant jilted lovers, lovesick blues and see-ya-later blues. I can't remember all of the titles now but I knew the songs as each of them began. "I Can't Stop Loving You," "Heartache by the Number," "You Ain't Woman Enough to Take My Man" were some of the songs we listened to. I was reminded by all of this of how important and formative music and books and art are in their impact on our moods, both in getting us in them and in getting us out of them.

One of my growing joys is the discovery of literary treasures from centuries and even millennia gone by. I know this experience is not unique to me. There has always been a trans-generational cross-pollenization process going on. Composers have seen pictures or read a piece of literature and then composed under the inspirational influence. Writers have also heard music or seen art and gained direction or inspiration for their work. Artists, while listening to great music or reading great literature, have been stirred to create their masterpieces, which then have been seen by composers or writers, and so on and so on.

I wonder if, while on pilgrimage here on earth, we have been careful to surround ourselves with music and art and literature that positively helps us on that journey? Do we let our environment shape us or do we shape our environment, via

121

music and books and art? Are we beavers—altering the terrain to accommodate us—or opossums—accommodating to the terrain as we find it?

Think for a moment. Do you regularly listen to a certain kind of music? Do you spend time listening to talk radio or watching talk shows? Do regularly read books? Or are you primarily a T.V. or movie watcher? Can you discern whether or not your loneliness is caused by or aggravated by or cured by certain influences that you can regulate, like music, art and literature?

It would be useless for me to give the reader my list of favorite music or books, when it comes to uplifting my feelings. But it is vitally important that the reader recognizes his or her own responsiveness to these phantom crutches. It is not only vital for one's own ability to make adjustments when loneliness is on the increase but also for those who may be helped by what we create during our lifetimes—both in the dark times and in the sunny times. The songs that grip you and cheer you with their sounds or the words that say things you have felt or thought but couldn't put into words were written by people who created them out of their life circumstances. The music or poem or portrait was the canvass they poured their hearts out on. You and I are the beneficiaries. We, too, have some part to play in spanning time and space to help someone through our creations, made during or made because of our lonely times.

Throughout these chapters I have scattered poems and readings. The cover picture was created by my daughter, Esther. Have any of these things provoked a positive response in you? Think of Lamentations 3:21–27 as a final example of how one person's dark experience, harnessed, can cross the chasm of time and be a bridge for others to cross more safely by.

The song "Great is Thy Faithfulness" was written by Thomas Chisolm in 1923. It was immediately embraced by believers as a favorite and its stock has not gone anywhere but up since then. He stated that the inspiration for the words came from his personal Bible study in Lamentation 3:21–27.

Mr. Runyan, a friend of Mr. Chisolm's and a member of the Moody Bible Institute family, was so taken by the words that he composed music especially for them. Who would have thought that such a solid, uplifting, doxological hymn could be derived from a book with a morose title like "Lamentations" and whose contents justify that morose title's appropriateness. But that lonely man, that abandoned and banished and attacked prophet, Jeremiah, experienced both the abysmal events of Jerusalem's downfall in 586 B.C. and the amazing comfort that God gave him, while sitting in the ashes and the gore of Jerusalem's rubble. Lamentations 3:21–27 occurred during the lowest point in the book of Lamentations, and it comes so shockingly sudden that it is breathtaking. It is almost like a bad joke and mournful funeral—bad timing or bad taste. But it is the unexpected nature of finding comfort and hope and purpose so close to pain and despair and confusion that explains the powerful impact on both Jeremiah and Mr. Chisolm, the lyricist. Out of his misery, out of the very blackest times of his misery, Jeremiah created something with words. God preserved them and gripped Mr. Chisolm with them 2400 years later. Mr. Runyan was moved by the words of Mr. Chisolm, based on Jeremiah's words, and added music to carry the message to untold millions, with the effect of indelibly etching the words of Jeremiah into our very souls. Does this musical medicine cure or curse? Save or kill? Fill or empty the heart?

This same principle could be illustrated and proven thousands and thousands of times, from both world history and from each of our personal histories. So let me inquire once more, what music do you frequently listen to, that lifts you out of a gloomy time? What books, what art, what phantom crutches have had the effect of filling the void in your soul?

Who have you found that needs your care, your creativity, your sage counsel and corny sense of humor? The loneliest people on earth are the ones who matter most only to themselves. They haven't found out yet that one of the secrets of life is to give it away if you want to keep it. Do we have a growing list of those who have hurt us, lied to us, abandoned us or neglected us, but a shrinking list of those we are caring for and serving? One has only to listen to which personal pronoun we most use—*"I, me, my" or " you, he, she, them*—to determine whether our loneliness is the healthy kind, leading to the divinely intended outcomes, or the twisted kind, resulting in filling Satan's empty heart with hollow joy and keeping us more hollow in the process.

INTERLUDE

A SUGGESTED PLAY LIST ON THE THEME OF LONELINESS

Compiled by pts

Tell Me the Story Again by Chris Rice
Far Country by Andrew Peterson
Don't Let Me Come Home a Stranger by Fernando Ortega
Pain That Plagues the Nations by Mark Heard
Empty by Michael Tait
No One Else by Fernando Ortega
My Shadow Companion by Bob Bennett
Walk in the Dark by Wayne Watson
Grand Canyon by Wayne Kirkpatrick
What Susan Said by Rich Mullins
Silence of God by Andrew Peterson
Older than the Rain by Michael Card
We Are Not as Strong by Rich Mullins
If I Flee by Fernando Ortega
Land of My Sojourn by Rich Mullins
He Will Listen to You by Mark Heard
Season in Your Path by Wayne Watson
On the Line by Fernando Ortega
Fill Our Empty Hearts by Benny Hester
Breakfast Table by Chris Rice
In the Valley by Sovereign Grace Music
Smile by Chris Rice
Angel Fire by Fernando Ortega

Tell Your Story by Out of the Grey
Put a Window in the Wall by Wayne Kirkpatrick
Where You Are by Cindy Morgan
Belong by Chris Rice
Hatching of a Heart by Rich Mullins
Somebody's Watching by Chris Rice
Hold Me by Benny Hester
Brace by Out of the Grey
Spare An Angel by Chris Rice
Place in This World by Wayne Kirkpatrick
I Will Bring You Home by Michael Card
Come Home by Cindy Morgan
Someday Face to Face by Billy Crockett
Mercy As the Rain by Billy Crockett
Come Unto Me by Sweet Honey in the Rock
I Am by Nicole C. Mullen
As the Ruin Falls by Phil Keaggy

EPILOGUE

THE END OR THE BEGINNING?
(YOUR CHOICE)

I once read a piece by C. S. Lewis in which he described the following dilemma. How could William Shakespeare, the writer, have fellowship with his literary characters, like Hamlet or Macbeth or Julius Caesar? Could he animate them in some way so as to make them walk off of the page and then sit and tell him how they would really have acted or what they really would have said? Or were they destined to be forever separate—the writer and the characters he wrote? Lewis went on to answer his question by asserting that the only way in which an author can really interact with his literary creations and they with him is to write himself into the story and let the real him meet and fellowship with the real, make believe characters in the plot. His point in this illustration, as strained as it may seem, was to illustrate what God has really done in the incarnation of the Son, Jesus Christ. What is impossible for us to imagine in the literary realm, and unutterably amazing in the spiritual realm—is that the Creator became a creature, the Author became a part of the cast of His tragedy/comedy/drama. Without losing His identity or essence as Creator, God really became a creature—a human fetus, to be exact. And He experienced all that humans do and all that God does, at the same time. This, of course, puts Him into a class by Himself, as mentioned in an earlier chapter.

The reason for mentioning this here, at the end of these meditations on loneliness, is to make the reader aware of the ocean of meditation that the incarnation of the Son is, if he or she will but reverse the tactic and enter in to the experience of Jesus Christ, as recorded in the Word. (*That's two, distinct steps: 1. examining the Word and 2. considering carefully the details of the life of Christ.*) In other words, how can a literary character that has met the author, who has written himself into the story, continue that communion when the author returns to his desk and continues to write the next chapters of the book? As before, only by reading and meditating on the part of the book where the author was actually living with him in the plot. There he will know what the author is really like and what he really believes and what he plans to do in the rest of the story. The very fact that he would enter the story at all, at great personal sacrifice, is an unutterable gift. And what sort of a role did he write for himself? Did he have a major role from the moment he appeared on the page? Was he handsome? Wealthy? Strong? Popular? Well educated? Did he live long and build buildings or marry a beautiful girl or conquer lands or start a movement or found an ism to perpetuate his teaching? Did he have an easy time, full of home movie highlights and a trophy case full of awards? Did endow a college or invent new technology? Did he excel in sports or explore strange lands? The person in the story can have real, living, enduring communion with the author even after the author has gone only by the power of reflection and recollection.

This is what we do when we read books from across the ages. The writer distilled his ideas into words and put them on the page. Long after he is no more his thoughts and feelings about whatever he wrote about are still there, ready for you and I to discover. When we do, our minds meet at the point of the words. True, it is a one way exchange in that we can't talk back and get him or her to respond. Nevertheless it is an exchange of ideas and that exchange can affect us in the present, into the future and into other lives that we will impact.

So back to Lewis' analogy. The reason why I am not writing a separate chapter on Jesus Christ's experience of loneliness is not because of lack of information but because of the abundance of information. I have sprinkled His name throughout the chapters as I went because, ultimately, the experience of the Author of life while on earth is the one meditation worth

128

cultivating and concentrating on, more than any other. His interaction with the other characters in the storyline reveals too much about our needs and His fullness for one chapter to adequately cover. So I am closing this work by inviting the reader to go to the Bible, Old and New Testaments, and enter into the experiences of God the Son through reading, reflection and meditation. The Holy Spirit was sent for this specific purpose, according to Jesus.

> *"These things I have spoken to you while being present with you. But the Helper, the Holy Spirit, whom the Father will send in My name, He will teach you all things, and bring to your remembrance all things that I said to you."*

—John 14:25, 26

> *"But when the Helper comes, whom I shall send to you from the Father, the Spirit of truth who proceeds from the Father, He will testify of Me."*

—John 15:26

> *"Nevertheless I tell you the truth. It is to your advantage that I go away; for if I do not go away, the Helper will not come to you; but if I depart, I will send Him to you. And when He has come, He will convict the world of sin, and of righteousness, and of judgment: of sin, because they do not believe in Me; of righteousness, because I go to My Father and you see Me no more; of judgment, because the ruler of this world is judged.*
>
> *I still have many things to say to you, but you cannot bear* them *now. However, when He, the Spirit of truth, has come, He will guide you into all truth; for He will not speak on His own* authority, *but whatever He hears He will speak; and He will tell you things to come. He will glorify Me, for He will take of what is Mine and declare* it *to you. All things that the Father has are Mine. Therefore I said that He will take of Mine and declare* it *to you."*

—John 16:7–11,13,14

What will you find if you do accept my invitation? What I have found has led me to conclude that Christ is what the Bible is all about. Some of the most amazing things about Him are tucked away in seldom traveled sections of the Old Testament, like Leviticus, the Psalms and the Prophets. Even conversations between the Father and the Son are recorded there, and no where else (Isa. 49:1–7, 50:4–11; Psalm 22)! It is unmistakably the case that the eternal Son entered into the whole range of human experiences, without being tainted with sin, as to His nature or His deeds, and that the Holy Spirit was pleased to record His life for us to enter into His fellowship. That record is not exhaustive, that is, the Scriptures do not tells us everything Jesus Christ said or did the entire time He was alive on earth. Rather, the record is selective, with God the Spirit recording what it pleased Him for us to know about the life of Author while He tabernacled among us (John 1:14).

What will you miss if you don't focus your mind on the Savior, in His past life, in His present glorious state or in His life that is to come? Among other things, and most relevant to this study on loneliness, you will have isolated yourself from God's greatest remedy for loneliness—both the original, designed type and the type resulting from sin. By ignoring God's greatest act in history you will have cursed yourself to being a stranger and outcast in the present and possibly forever. When He pronounces, *"Depart from Me, I never knew you,"* you will then realize that He is only quoting your own words to Him, uttered every time you closed the Book or filled your mind with other things but Him. The soul that feels itself deserted, abandoned, isolated, and alone may, in fact, be the one who does the deserting, abandoning, isolating and excluding.

The Author, the Creator, the Judge has offered Himself to us now, to accompany us throughout our lifetime, through everything that comes our way. He has all the credentials to make His presence infinitely desirable and critical. Will we welcome Him in?

The great hope we live upon, as believers, is that He who once made everything and then entered into the world He had made as one of the creatures will return to live with us forever—the Author with the characters—in holy, unbroken, untainted, unparalleled fellowship. We will be no more strangers and pilgrims, often alone and in despair. We will be Home, with the other saved sinners of all time, with the unfallen angels, and with the incarnate Author.

POSTLUDE

"I am the Lord your God, who has separated you from the peoples."

—Leviticus 20:24

"And you shall be holy to Me, for I the Lord am holy, and have separated you from the peoples, that you should be Mine."

—Leviticus 20:26

"Who shall separate us from the love of Christ? Shall tribulation, or distress, or persecution, or famine, or nakedness, or peril, or sword? As it is written: 'For Your sake we are killed all day long; We are accounted as sheep for the slaughter.' Yet in all these things we are more than conquerors through Him who loved us. For I am persuaded that neither death nor life, nor angels nor principalities nor powers, nor things present nor things to come, nor height nor depth, nor any other created thing, shall be able to separate us from the love of God which is in Christ Jesus our Lord."

—Romans 8:35–39

"Now I saw a new heaven and a new earth, for the first heaven and first earth had passed away. Also there was no more sea. Then I, John, saw the holy city, New Jerusalem, coming down out of heaven from God, prepared as a bride adorned for her husband. And I heard a loud voice from heaven saying, "Behold, the tabernacle of God is with

132

men, and He will dwell with them, and they shall be His people. God Himself will be with them and be *their God. And God will wipe away every tear from their eyes; there shall be no more death, nor sorrow, nor crying. There shall be no more pain, for the former things have passed away."*

But I saw no temple in it, for the Lord God Almighty and the Lamb are its temple. The city had no need of the sun or of the moon to shine in it, for the glory of God illuminated it. The Lamb is *its light. And the nations of those who are saved shall walk in its light, and the kings of the earth bring their glory and honor into it. Its gates shall not be shut at all by day (there shall be no night there). And they shall bring the glory and the honor of the nations into it. But there shall by no means enter it anything that defiles, or causes an abomination or a lie, but only those who are written in the Lamb's Book of Life.*

—**Revelation 21**

And he showed me a pure river of water of life, clear as crystal, proceeding from the throne of God and of the Lamb. In the middle of its street, and on either side of the river, was *the tree of life, which bore twelve fruits, each* tree *yielding its fruit every month. The leaves of the tree* were *for the healing of the nations. And there shall be no more curse, but the throne of God and of the Lamb shall be in it, and His servants shall serve Him. They shall see His face, and His name* shall be *on their foreheads. There shall be no night there: They need no lamp nor light of the sun, for the Lord God gives them light. And they shall reign forever and ever.*

"And behold, I am coming quickly, and My reward is *with Me, to give to every one according to his work. I am the Alpha and the Omega,* the *Beginning and* the *End, the First and the Last." Blessed* are *those who do His commandments, that they may have the right to the tree of life, and may enter through the gates into the city. But outside* are *dogs and sorcerers and sexually immoral and murderers and idolaters, and whoever loves and practices*

a lie. "I, Jesus, have sent My angel to testify to you these things in the churches. I am the Root and the Offspring of David, the Bright and Morning Star."

And the Spirit and the bride say, "Come!" And let him who hears say, "Come!" And let him who thirsts come. Whoever desires, let him take the water of life freely. For I testify to everyone who hears the words of the prophecy of this book: If anyone adds to these things, God will add to him the plagues that are written in this book; and if anyone takes away from the words of the book of this prophecy, God shall take away his part from the Book of Life, from the holy city, and from *the things which are written in this book. He who testifies to these things says, "Surely I am coming quickly." Amen. Even so, come, Lord Jesus! The grace of our Lord Jesus Christ* be *with you all. Amen.*

—**Revelation 22**

CHAPTER REVIEWS

Chapter 1: Lonely by Design

Why, then, did God, in His wisdom, create what He knew to be inadequate or unsuitable from the outset? And after announcing His assessment of Adam's solitude (2:18) why did God set him about the task of naming the animals? (2:18,19) Was He hoping that maybe the other creatures would fill the emptiness Adam felt? Did He think that the animals could fulfill Adam and achieve the "good" label the rest of creation had in His eyes? Was God experimenting?

- God created man lonely, by design, to bring him to want Himself, to love Him, to glorify Him for His glorious virtues (power, wisdom, goodness, etc.).

- Mankind's sin has magnified and aggravated the original, designed loneliness by alienating us from God, darkening our understanding, perverting our emotions and exposing us to being pillaged by the world, the flesh and the devil. (Eph. 4:17–20)

- What we have now, since Genesis 3 is <u>double loneliness</u>: *designed loneliness*, which was meant to find fulfillment in God's provision of companionship and *fallen loneliness*, which has destroyed the foundation of all created fulfillment by alienating God from all friendly and loving fellowship with us.

Chapter 2: Headwaters and Tailwaters

Adam and Eve were the headwaters of all humankind, according to the wisdom of God. He didn't make a bunch of people, like He did animals. He made one pair, investing their behavior under the covenant He made with them with a profound significance for all the "downriver" descendants they carried in their bodies. Both due to their physical/ genetic parentage and to their representative placement over God's earthly creation (Gen. 1:26–31) their actions would either pollute or maintain the purity of their original righteousness for all of their offspring (Rom. 5:12–21; Eccl. 7:29).

God did not completely abandon His creation after Adam sinned. His alienation is not absolute but it is real. He is the offended, infinitely holy One, and it is His great power to restrain His wrath that appears most glorious in this post-Fall world. The subsequent history of redemption reveals His ongoing presence and activity among the broken shards of that once perfect stained glass window. He has undertaken to purify the *tailwaters* by diverting them into a *new headwater*—Christ.

Chapter 3: An Empty Well, Filled

Human companionship alone is insufficient to satisfy the deep thirst of our souls. No matter how much or how many we accumulate, no created thing can produce absolute fullness in us. He alone can satisfy the infinite hunger we have. This is for our good and to His glory.

Chapter 4: A Full Well, Emptied

Solomon's life reveals a side of loneliness that has similarities to Adam's story. Both had incredible assets to start out with, and yet both squandered their riches and those of their posterity by pursuing what God had forbidden. Both, taken together, put to death the lie that prosperity is the cure for loneliness. Those who have abundance of material goods, intellectual attainments or human companions are no more likely to be content and satisfied with that wealth than those in the exact opposite condition—alone on a desert island.

From this we should expand our view of loneliness to include some of those people who attempt to fill the contentment void by shopping, collecting, micro-managing their own life or the lives of others, travel incessantly or have a burgeoning social life. They may be dealing with the pangs of loneliness rather than living the good life we imagined they had.

Chapter 5: Lone Rangers

The pangs of loneliness, while very real, are not uncontrollable and should not be in control of our lives. **Neither prophet became the victim of his circumstances.** They struggled, yes. But they struggled falling forward.

The ways we experience human companionship are more varied than just marriage or friendship. In these two cases I see companionship expressed or withheld by the family unit, a hometown population, civic and national leaders, servants and national populations. Each, in their own way, provides some measure of our need for a sense of belonging, not to the exclusion of a mate or close friendships, but as supplements to them. There are a variety of ways our hunger for companionship should be and can be addressed. All of them together cannot render me immune to loneliness. That's the lesson of Solomon. Nor can any one of them being absent condemn me to bondage to loneliness. That's the lesson of Jeremiah and Ezekiel.

Chapter 6: Moses—Alone in a Crowd

His words only underscore two profound truths: (1) <u>no one is immune to despair</u> and (2) <u>one can be very much alone in a crowd</u>.

Moses' loneliness—a responsible person's loneliness—was the result of continual, extreme, and sometimes exotic demands placed upon him by his followers or dependents. Even if he or she is married and has family and friends to accompany him or her in life, the position may be so overwhelming that they become isolated, in their own minds. She may feel walled in. He may develop a martyr complex. "Woe is me" may be his frequent, unstated utterance. Or she may consider suicide as an alternative to living under such conditions. And the manifestation of this loneliness may be anger, directed at others, especially God.

Chapter 7: Displaced Persons

There is a gravitation or magnetism toward those who share our interests and experiences and a converse repulsion or distancing from those who are unlike us, who can't understand from experience what our life is like.

So one thing we should be doing regularly is stockpiling our minds with detailed awareness of the life of Jesus Christ while He was on earth. The more we know and meditate on His experience among us the better able we will be to find in Him an understanding and strong priest.

Chapter 8: Of Angels and Demons

Angels and men experience loneliness, estrangement, emptiness, vanity. All who are victims of sin are partakers of sin's consequences, and that includes sin's first casualty, Satan.

The unholy angels are both the instruments that aggravate human misery and loneliness (even to the point of everlasting banishment) and also the sufferers of loneliness themselves. The holy angels are also both instruments and participants in human fulfillment. They are appointed as the guardians of saved sinners (Heb. 1:14; Matt. 18:10) and only in their company will our full blessedness be experienced.

Chapter 9: Phantom Crutches

Can you discern whether or not your loneliness is caused by or aggravated by or cured by certain influences that you can regulate, like music, art and literature?

The songs that grip you and cheer you with their sounds or the words that say things you have felt or thought but couldn't put into words were written by people who created them out of their life circumstances. The music or poem or portrait was the canvass they poured their hearts out on. You and I are the beneficiaries. We, too, have some part to play in spanning time and space to help someone through our creations, made during or made because of our lonely times.

APPENDIX

[The following is an excerpt from Augustine's personal biography, written when he was the bishop of the town of Hippo, in North Africa. This is a profound insight into several areas of concern in this study of loneliness.]

CHAPTER IV/ BOOK 4—CONFESSIONS OF ST. AUGUSTINE

"7. In those years, when I first began to teach rhetoric in my native town, I had gained a very dear friend, about my own age, who was associated with me in the same studies. Like myself, he was just rising up into the flower of youth. He had grown up with me from childhood and we had been both school fellows and playmates. But he was not then my friend, nor indeed ever became my friend, in the true sense of the term; for there is no true friendship save between those thou dost bind together and who cleave to thee by that love which is "shed abroad in our hearts through the Holy Spirit who is given to us." Still, it was a sweet friendship, being ripened by the zeal of common studies. Moreover, I had turned him away from the true faith—which he had not soundly and thoroughly mastered as a youth—and turned him toward those superstitious and harmful fables which my mother mourned in me. With me this man went wandering off in error and my soul could not exist without him. But behold thou wast close behind thy fugitives—at once a God of vengeance and a Fountain of mercies, who dost turn us to

140

thyself by ways that make us marvel. Thus, thou didst take that man out of this life when he had scarcely completed one whole year of friendship with me, sweeter to me than all the sweetness of my life thus far.

8. Who can show forth all thy praise for that which he has experienced in himself alone? What was it that thou didst do at that time, O my God; how unsearchable are the depths of thy judgments! For when, sore sick of a fever, he long lay unconscious in a death sweat and everyone despaired of his recovery, he was baptized without his knowledge. And I myself cared little, at the time, presuming that his soul would retain what it had taken from me rather than what was done to his unconscious body. It turned out, however, far differently, for he was revived and restored. Immediately, as soon as I could talk to him—and I did this as soon as he was able, for I never left him and we hung on each other overmuch—I tried to jest with him, supposing that he also would jest in return about that baptism which he had received when his mind and senses were inactive, but which he had since learned that he had received. But he recoiled from me, as if I were his enemy, and, with a remarkable and unexpected freedom, he admonished me that, if I desired to continue as his friend, I must cease to say such things. Confounded and confused, I concealed my feelings till he should get well and his health recover enough to allow me to deal with him as I wished. But he was snatched away from my madness, that with thee he might be preserved for my consolation. A few days after, during my absence, the fever returned and he died.

9. My heart was utterly darkened by this sorrow and everywhere I looked I saw death. My native place was a torture room to me and my father's house a strange unhappiness. And all the things I had done with him—now that he was gone— became a frightful torment. My eyes sought him everywhere, but they did not see him; and I hated all places because he was not in them, because they could not say to me, "Look, he is coming," as they did when he was alive and absent. I became a hard riddle to myself, and I asked my soul why she was so downcast and why this disquieted me so sorely. But she did not know how to answer me. And if I said, "Hope thou in God, she very properly

141

disobeyed me, because that dearest friend she had lost was as an actual man, both truer and better than the imagined deity she was ordered to put her hope in. Nothing but tears were sweet to me and they took my friend's place in my heart's desire.

10. But now, O Lord, these things are past and time has healed my wound. Let me learn from thee, who art Truth, and put the ear of my heart to thy mouth, that thou mayest tell me why weeping should be so sweet to the unhappy. Hast thou—though omnipresent—dismissed our miseries from thy concern? Thou abidest in thyself while we are disquieted with trial after trial. Yet unless we wept in thy ears, there would be no hope for us remaining. How does it happen that such sweet fruit is plucked from the bitterness of life, from groans, tears, sighs, and lamentations? Is it the hope that thou wilt hear us that sweetens it? This is true in the case of prayer, for in a prayer there is a desire to approach thee. But is it also the case in grief for a lost love, and in the kind of sorrow that had then overwhelmed me? For I had neither a hope of his coming back to life, nor in all my tears did I seek this. I simply grieved and wept, for I was miserable and had lost my joy. Or is weeping a bitter thing that gives us pleasure because of our aversion to the things we once enjoyed and this only as long as we loathe them?

11. But why do I speak of these things? Now is not the time to ask such questions, but rather to confess to thee. I was wretched; and every soul is wretched that is fettered in the friendship of mortal things—it is torn to pieces when it loses them, and then realizes the misery which it had even before it lost them. Thus it was at that time with me. I wept most bitterly, and found a rest in bitterness. I was wretched, and yet that wretched life I still held dearer than my friend. For though I would willingly have changed it, I was still more unwilling to lose it than to have lost him. Indeed, I doubt whether I was willing to lose it, even for him—as they tell (unless it be fiction) of the friendship of Orestes and Pylades; they would have gladly died for one another, or both together, because not to love together was worse than death to them. But a strange kind of feeling had come over me, quite different from this, for now it was wearisome to live and a fearful thing to die. I suppose that the

more I loved him the more I hated and feared, as the most cruel enemy, that death which had robbed me of him. I even imagined that it would suddenly annihilate all men, since it had had such a power over him. This is the way I remember it was with me.

Look into my heart, O God! Behold and look deep within me, for I remember it well, O my Hope who cleansest me from the uncleanness of such affections, directing my eyes toward thee and plucking my feet out of the snare. And I marveled that other mortals went on living since he whom I had loved as if he would never die was now dead. And I marveled all the more that I, who had been a second self to him, could go on living when he was dead. Someone spoke rightly of his friend as being "his soul's other half"—for I felt that my soul and his soul were but one soul in two bodies. Consequently, my life was now a horror to me because I did not want to live as a half self. But it may have been that I was afraid to die, lest he should then die wholly whom I had so greatly loved.

12. O madness that knows not how to love men as they should be loved! O foolish man that I was then, enduring with so much rebellion the lot of every man! Thus I fretted, sighed, wept, tormented myself, and took neither rest nor counsel, for I was dragging around my torn and bloody soul. It was impatient of my dragging it around, and yet I could not find a place to lay it down. Not in pleasant groves, nor in sport or song, nor in fragrant bowers, nor in magnificent banquetings, nor in the pleasures of the bed or the couch; not even in books or poetry did it find rest. All things looked gloomy, even the very light itself. Whatsoever was not what he was, was now repulsive and hateful, except my groans and tears, for in those alone I found a little rest. But when my soul left off weeping, a heavy burden of misery weighed me down. It should have been raised up to thee, O Lord, for thee to lighten and to lift. This I knew, but I was neither willing nor able to do; especially since, in my thoughts of thee, thou wast not thyself but only an empty fantasm. Thus my error was my god. If I tried to cast off my burden on this fantasm, that it might find rest there, it sank through the vacuum and came rushing down again upon me. Thus I remained to myself an unhappy lodging where I could neither stay nor leave.

For where could my heart fly from my heart? Where could I fly from my own self? Where would I not follow myself? And yet I did flee from my native place so that my eyes would look for him less in a place where they were not accustomed to see him. Thus I left the town of Tagaste and returned to Carthage."

13. Time never lapses, nor does it glide at leisure through our sense perceptions. It does strange things in the mind. Lo, time came and went from day to day, and by coming and going it brought to my mind other ideas and remembrances, and little by little they patched me up again with earlier kinds of pleasure and my sorrow yielded a bit to them. But yet there followed after this sorrow, not other sorrows just like it, but the causes of other sorrows. For why had that first sorrow so easily penetrated to the quick except that I had poured out my soul onto the dust, by loving a man as if he would never die who nevertheless had to die? What revived and refreshed me, more than anything else, was the consolation of other friends, with whom I went on loving the things I loved instead of thee. This was a monstrous fable and a tedious lie which was corrupting my soul with its "itching ears" by its adulterous rubbing. And that fable would not die to me as often as one of my friends died. And there were other things in our companionship that took strong hold of my mind: to discourse and jest with him; to indulge in courteous exchanges; to read pleasant books together; to trifle together; to be earnest together; to differ at times without ill-humor, as a man might do with himself, and even through these infrequent dissensions to find zest in our more frequent agreements; sometimes teaching, sometimes being taught; longing for someone absent with impatience and welcoming the homecomer with joy. These and similar tokens of friendship, which spring spontaneously from the hearts of those who love and are loved in return—in countenance, tongue, eyes, and a thousand ingratiating gestures—were all so much fuel to melt our souls together, and out of the many made us one.

14. This is what we love in our friends, and we love it so much that a man's conscience accuses itself if he does not love one who loves him, or respond in love to love, seeking nothing from the other but the evidences of his love. **This is the source**

of our moaning when one dies—the gloom of sorrow, the steeping of the heart in tears, all sweetness turned to bitterness—and the feeling of death in the living, because of the loss of the life of the dying.

Blessed is he who loves thee, and who loves his friend in Thee, and his enemy also, for Thy sake; for he alone loses none dear to him, if all are dear in Him who cannot be lost. And who is this but our God: the God that created heaven and earth, and filled them because he created them by filling them up? None loses Thee but he who leaves Thee; and he who leaves Thee, where does he go, or where can he flee but from Thee well-pleased to Thee offended? For where does he not find Thy law fulfilled in his own punishment? "Thy law is the truth" and thou art Truth.

15. Turn us again, O Lord God of Hosts, cause thy face to shine; and we shall be saved." For wherever the soul of man turns itself, unless toward thee, it is enmeshed in sorrows, even though it is surrounded by beautiful things outside thee and outside itself. For lovely things would simply not be unless they were from thee. They come to be and they pass away, and by coming they begin to be, and they grow toward perfection. Then, when perfect, they begin to wax old and perish, and, if all do not wax old, still all perish. Therefore, when they rise and grow toward being, the more rapidly they grow to maturity, so also the more rapidly they hasten back toward nonbeing. This is the way of things. This is the lot thou hast given them, because they are part of things which do not all exist at the same time, but by passing away and succeeding each other they all make up the universe, of which they are all parts. For example, our speech is accomplished by sounds which signify meanings, but a meaning is not complete unless one word passes away, when it has sounded its part, so that the next may follow after it. Let my soul praise thee, in all these things, O God, the Creator of all; but let not my soul be stuck to these things by the glue of love, through the senses of the body. For they go where they were meant to go, that they may exist no longer. And they rend the soul with pestilent desires because she longs to be and yet loves to rest secure in the created things she

loves. But in these things there is no resting place to be found. They do not abide. They flee away; and who is he who can follow them with his physical senses? Or who can grasp them, even when they are present? For our physical sense is slow because it is a physical sense and bears its own limitations in itself. The physical sense is quite sufficient for what it was made to do; but it is not sufficient to stay things from running their courses from the beginning appointed to the end appointed. For in thy word, by which they were created, they hear their appointed bound: "From there—to here!"

16. Be not foolish, O my soul, and do not let the tumult of your vanity deafen the ear of your heart. Be attentive. The Word itself calls you to return, and with him is a place of unperturbed rest, where love is not forsaken unless it first forsakes. Behold, these things pass away that others may come to be in their place. Thus even this lowest level of unite may be made complete in all its parts. "But do I ever pass away?" asks the Word of God. Fix your habitation in him. O my soul, commit whatsoever you have to him. For at long last you are now becoming tired of deceit. Commit to truth whatever you have received from the truth, and you will lose nothing. What is decayed will flourish again; your diseases will be healed; your perishable parts shall be reshaped and renovated, and made whole again in you. And these perishable things will not carry you with them down to where they go when they perish, but shall stand and abide, and you with them, before God, who abides and continues forever.

17. Why then, my perverse soul, do you go on following your flesh? Instead, let it be converted so as to follow you. Whatever you feel through it is but partial. You do not know the whole, of which sensations are but parts; and yet the parts delight you. But if my physical senses had been able to comprehend the whole—and had not as a part of their punishment received only a portion of the whole as their own province—you would then desire that whatever exists in the present time should also pass away so that the whole might please you more. For what we speak, you also hear through physical sensation, and yet you would not wish that the syllables

should remain. Instead, you wish them to fly past so that others may follow them, and the whole be heard. Thus it is always that when any single thing is composed of many parts which do not coexist simultaneously, the whole gives more delight than the parts could ever do perceived separately. But far better than all this is He who made it all. He is our God and he does not pass away, for there is nothing to take his place.

18. If physical objects please you, praise God for them, but turn back your love to their Creator, lest, in those things which please you, you displease him. If souls please you, let them be loved in God; for in themselves they are mutable, but in him firmly established—without him they would simply cease to exist. In him, then, let them be loved; and bring along to him with yourself as many souls as you can, and say to them: "Let us love him, for he himself created all these, and he is not far away from them. For he did not create them and then go away. They are of him and in him. Behold, there he is, wherever truth is known. He is within the inmost heart, yet the heart has wandered away from him. Return to your heart, O you transgressors, and hold fast to him who made you. Stand with him and you shall stand fast. Rest in him and you shall be at rest. Where do you go along these rugged paths? Where are you going? The good that you love is from him, and insofar as it is also for him, it is both good and pleasant. But it will rightly be turned to bitterness if whatever comes from him is not rightly loved and if he is deserted for the love of the creature. Why then will you wander farther and farther in these difficult and toilsome ways? There is no rest where you seek it. Seek what you seek; but remember that it is not where you seek it. You seek for a blessed life in the land of death. It is not there. For how can there be a blessed life where life itself is not?"

19. But our very Life came down to earth and bore our death, and slew it with the very abundance of his own life. And, thundering, he called us to return to him into that secret place from which he came forth to us—coming first into the virginal womb, where the human creature, our mortal flesh, was joined to him that it might not be forever mortal—and came "as a bridegroom coming out his chamber, rejoicing as a strong man

to run a race. For he did not delay, but ran through the world, crying out by words, deeds, death, life, descent, ascension—crying aloud to us to return to him. And he departed from our sight that we might return to our hearts and find him there. For he left us, and behold, he is here. He could not be with us long, yet he did not leave us. He went back to the place that he had never left, for "the world was made by him." In this world he was, and into this world he came, to save sinners. To him my soul confesses, and he heals it, because it had sinned against him. O sons of men, how long will you be so slow of heart? Even now after Life itself has come down to you, will you not ascend and live? But where will you climb if you are already on a pinnacle and have set your mouth against the heavens? First come down that you may climb up, climb up to God. For you have fallen by trying to climb against him. Tell this to the souls you love that they may weep in the valley of tears, and so bring them along with you to God, because it is by his spirit that you speak thus to them, if, as you speak, you burn with the fire of love.

20. These things I did not understand at that time, and I loved those inferior beauties, and I was sinking down to the very depths. And I said to my friends: "Do we love anything but the beautiful? What then is the beautiful? And what is beauty? What is it that allures and unites us to the things we love; for unless there were a grace and beauty in them, they could not possibly attract us to them?" And I reflected on this and saw that in the objects themselves there is a kind of beauty which comes from their forming a whole and another kind of beauty that comes from mutual fitness—as the harmony of one part of the body with its whole, or a shoe with a foot, and so on. And this idea sprang up in my mind out of my inmost heart, and I wrote some books—two or three, I think—*On the Beautiful and the Fitting*. Thou knowest them, O Lord; they have escaped my memory. I no longer have them; somehow they have been mislaid.

Made in the USA
Middletown, DE
31 October 2024